Cruise
THE MEDITERRANEAN

Dedicated to Rosie,
my dearly beloved wife
and best friend – many happy, shared,
memories
– – – – – – – – –

Published by
The P&R Agency Ltd
4, Sewells Farm, Birdshole Lane, Barcombe
Near Lewes, East Sussex BN8 5TJ

FOREWORD

I have been fortunate to have been involved with cruising for the last twelve years and have seen first hand the growth in its popularity. One reason for this could be the fact that, of necessity, airports have become increasingly less user-friendly and the cruise lines have capitalised on this opportunity, going out of their way to make their products more varied, more exciting, and much better valued. But I think that the principal reason is because the world at large is awakening to the sheer joy of cruising – there is nothing quite like browsing through glossy brochures that speak eloquently of far away places, learning about the astonishing facilities offered on the modern cruiseship, and then discovering that, above all, the cruise is absolutely affordable, no longer the preserve of the very rich. A modern cruise provides an opportunity to see new places with a minimum of fuss – and one can do so whilst being cosseted and protected by a luxurious floating hotel; and the modern cruiseship will meet the demands of even the most discerning and discriminating holiday-maker. The only criticism that I've encountered in many years is – 'one day in a particular place is not enough' – and this criticism is valid, because the average stay in port is less than twelve hours.

Twelve years serving as a 'Destination' Lecturer on many of the world's leading cruise lines have taught me what a passenger can reasonably expect to see during (an admittedly brief) stay. On arriving at a port one is faced with two choices: opt for one of the ship's organised excursions, or 'go it alone' and visit the place independently. Organised excursions are fine but they can be expensive and over the duration of a cruise their cost adds up, whereas 'going it alone' presents a dilemma – where to go, and what to see. One can of course refer to a guide book to that particular place, or one can consult a much slimmer volume prepared specifically for the cruise passenger: the former will overwhelm with information because it's been prepared for someone spending some time in the place, whereas the latter will likely be rather sketchy, because the publisher is concerned with packing as many ports as possible into a manageable book.

This book falls between these two ends of the spectrum, providing a great deal more information than the bespoke 'cruise' guide but considerably less than the 'conventional' guide. The content is tailored to the specific needs of the cruise passenger, and encompasses that which is relevant and achievable within the time frame of an average cruise visit.

I hope it enhances your cruise!

Peter Rushton, Sussex, 2009

PORTS
VISITED

Vigo, Spain - 5

Lisbon, Portugal - 13

Cadiz, Spain - 25

Malaga Spain - 33

Palma, Majorca - 43

Barcelona, Spain - 53

Livorno (for Florence), Italy - 63

Naples, Italy - 79

Straits of Messina - 90

Corfu, Greece - 91

Dubrovnik, Croatia - 101

Valletta, Malta - 111

Gibraltar - 123

VIGO
Spain

View over Harbour

Colegiata de Santa Maria

The Oyster Market

Statues, Gran Via

Horses

Fishermen

Cies Islands

VIGO
Gateway to Santiago

Vigo lies on the Atlantic coast of Spain, more or less mid-way between Cape Finisterre, the very northwestern tip of the Iberian Peninsular and the Portuguese border which is only about twenty miles away. This part of Spain is called Galicia and its coastline is characterised by wide, granite inlets called 'rias', with the district in the vicinity of Vigo itself known as the Rias Atlas.

As a whole, Galicia differs from the popular perception of Spain, and really is more akin to the Atlantic coasts of Ireland, Cornwall and Brittany than to places like, say, Malaga and Marbella.
Its people, too, are of very mixed origin – the Celtic tribes that first lived here were subdued in turn by the Romans, the Suevi, the Visigoths, the Normans and the Arabs. Then, in the Middle Ages, nearby Santiago de Compostela became one of the three principal places of Christian pilgrimage (the others being Jerusalem and Rome), and many peoples of far distant cultures came here as pilgrims and stayed, adding to the hodge podge of peoples and contributing to the creation of a race unique to the region. Look on any map and you can see the close proximity of Portugal, and the local language is very much a dialect of mixed Portuguese and Spanish with all traces of the original Celtic tongue lost to the mists of time.

Although the landscape is rugged, because of the mild, humid climate the vegetation is luxuriant and the hillsides are well wooded with evergreens like laurel, Ilex, chestnut, eucalyptus and maritime pine. Apple, pear and cherry orchards abound and the whole place is a bit of a wonderland, really, and certainly worth much more than a passing glance.
The estuary of the Ria del Vigo is dotted with islands and the town itself lies about six miles from the sea with the passage upstream interesting and worth getting up early to see – although you need to remember that in all probability your arrival will be timed for around 8 am. so you'd have to be on deck at about 7am to see the pilot embark.

Petroglyphs found among the stones of the nearby hills testify to an ancient habitation, and ruins of fortified villages speak of a people who defended their homes from invaders way back in prehistoric times: but we are really more concerned with the Vigo of today, so we'll leave the ancient history to the scholars who love to delve midst dusty archives.

The town owes a great deal to its maritime past, and many of its people have always made their living from the sea: some as fishermen, some as sailors in the Armada, some as seamen in the great ships that clashed with Nelson's "Victory" at Trafalgar in October, 1805.

Two hundred and twenty years before that historic conflict yet others defended their town from attacks by Sir Francis Drake (in 1585 and again in 1589) – so they are a hardy lot, and well used to people visiting them on ships. Often those visitors have been less friendly than we are and in the mid seventeenth century the locals fortified the city with a wall, most of which was demolished from 1860 onwards when urban development was the watchword: today there are very few traces of the wall remaining.

The Cruise Terminal, or "Estacion Maritima", is no more than a ten minute walk at most from the old part of town. (Those who don't feel like walking so early in the morning will be pleased to know that taxis are always available on the quayside). The terminal building is not awesome, but is functional and recognisable. There is a Tourist Information Office nearby and the pedestrianised shopping street called Calle Principe is close at hand.

The old town lies on the slopes of a hill that is home to two ancient fortresses, the Castillo de San Sebastian and the Castillo del Castro – the first about half way up, the second at the top. San Sebastian offers little of interest and has at any event been eclipsed by a ghastly concrete structure which houses the city's administrative offices, but there are fine views from the pleasant gardens surrounding del Castro.

Lovers of churches will find several in the town, but the principal one is the "Colegiata de Santa Maria" very close to the docks: built to commemorate the defeat of the French in the Peninsular War of 1808 – 1814, it is in the Gothic style, and stands near Constitution Square, the hub of the old city.

Walk eastwards from here through the rather fascinating streets and before long you'll find an extraordinary monument called 'El Sireno de Paco Leiro', a work created in cast metal which depicts an enormous fish with the face of a man. This stands in a street called Porta del Sol, very close to Prazza Princesca, just one of a number of attractive squares that are dotted about. Monuments and statues abound: still walking eastwards you'll reach the foot of the Gran Via, the main thoroughfare that runs through the heart of the modern city, and here you'll encounter 'The Fishermens' Statue', its massively muscled men forever hauling on their bursting nets. Heading southwards from this point is Gran Via, a modern, tree-lined street, flanked by major shops, banks, hotels and offices. At its highest point is Prazza de Espana, home to another monument, this time a particularly striking one popularly called 'Los Coballos' (the 'Horses') which was created by a sculptor called Jean Oliviera.

On every cruise to Spain that I have ever been on, many passengers make a beeline for the local equivalent to Marks & Spencer – El Corte

Inglés: well, the shoppers amongst you will be pleased to know that the Vigo branch is situated on Gran Via, halfway between the 'Fishermens' and the 'Horses' statues. El Corte is about a twenty five minute walk from the Cruise Terminal, and those wanting to make the most of their time there might be well advised to take a taxi. Often 'El Corte' will employ pretty girls on the quayside to hand out city maps and coupons which entitle cruise passengers visiting the shop to enjoy a free cup of coffee or glass of wine: these are quite genuine, and I have enjoyed several glasses of Rioja whilst waiting for my wife to browse the goodies on offer in the store. Good buys here are leather goods and ceramics, and Vigo is quite well known for its colourful shawls. Remember, that in Spain the currency is the Euro, and whether you intend to spend a lot or a little you'll need some of them for things like taxis and cups of coffee – although major credit cards are accepted just about everywhere else.

Just off Gran Via, near the top and not far from the Horses Statue stands another striking monument in a square called the Prazza Del Riego: as I said a little earlier, this is a city of monuments. Walking northwestwards from the Prazza Espana you'll reach the Parque do Castro – green and shady gardens that surround the Castillo of the same name. From here there are lovely views of the old city, over the harbour and your cruiseship, across the estuary to the distant shores and the open sea. The view is marred a little by the concrete town hall which towers like a sore thumb from the vicinity of Castillo San Sebastian half way down the hill, but it doesn't detract too much and if you ignore it you'll still enjoy the panorama. At the very top and in the grounds of the Castillo stands a rather grand restaurant whose plate glass windows afford diners an even better view.

Back in the old town, near the Cathedral is the street of the basket makers, the Calle do los Cesiteros – and a basket purchased here could be a good memento of your visit.

In my introduction I mentioned Vigo's fishermen. Very close to the Cruise Terminal is an excellent fishmarket where oysters are a speciality: behind the stalls that line the market are several cafés and restaurants, many of them frequented by the locals (always a good sign!), and in these you can take a seat whilst the ladies working on the stalls outside prepare your chosen oysters for you. Now, I don't know if you like oysters, but I can promise you that if you do, the ones served here are excellent! For your reference, the fish market is in a street called the Rua do Mestre Mateo.

Vigo is a place of contrasts – fine modern streets like Gran Via, with its splendid shops and major department stores – El Cortes is but one – through exclusive jewellers and up-market boutiques, many of them sited in the myriad of little, old, twisty back streets which characterise the older parts of town. There are several attractive parks in which to while away a pleasant hour. I've already told about the Parque Do Castro, but the main one, the Municipal Park of Quenones de Leon, is a short taxi ride to the south, not far from Praza America, the southwestern end of Gran Via. The park is home to the city's Open-Air Theatre and the Provincial Museum, housed in an imposing 17th Century mansion that is well worth a visit. The local culture is varied and quite unique, and I hope that the brief overview of the town itself has served to whet your appetite!

Vigo is a popular cruise destination these days, and is worth spending a little time on for, in my opinion, it is a pleasant place. But because of its popularity as a destination, you might well have been here before and want something different. Although this book is primarily intended for the independent traveller, there are some places that cannot be left out, and one of those is Santiago de Compostela, which has been a honeypot for visitors since long before the first guide book was ever written. Your cruise will certainly be offering a tour here, so if you have explored Vigo before and want to venture further afield then do consider the offer; of course, you can always take a taxi and see it for yourself, but do remember to establish the fare (there and back!) before embarking.

Sanitago is dominated by the absolutely stunning Cathedral which was built to commemorate the find, back in the 9th Century, of the body of Christ's apostle James. Originally built in the 12th Century Romanesque style, the building has a much later, and highly ornate, Obradoiro, façade.

It is awesome, not only because of its sheer size, but also because of its opulence: a mass of intricate carving, magnificent stained glass and gigantic naves, everything about it is on a truly colossal scale that is nothing short of magnificent – even the incense burner is mammoth, and if you take the tour you'll probably see it in action. Called the Bota Fumero, it requires several strong men to swing it

Surrounding the Cathedral are other imposing and picturesque squares, the most important of which is the Prazza Obradoiro: others are the Prazza Fonseca and the Prazza de Platerias (square of the silversmiths), named after the tradesmen who hammered out their religious icons for the streams of pilgrims who came, and still come, here.

The former Royal Palace, today the Ayuntamiento (Town Hall) of Santiago, is worthy of note as is the Hostal de los Reyes Catolicos, built as a home for pilgrims but today a five star hotel: if you take the all day, all inclusive tour that is almost certain to be on offer, you'll probably enjoy your lunch here – and a fine setting it is, too. Look out, too, for the Palace of St. Jerome.

Vehicles are not allowed into the heart of this ancient place so you'll have to de-bus some distance from the centre, and this will mean that you are going to be faced with some walking: also, be advised that those in wheel-chairs or with mobility problems will find access into the Cathedral difficult.

Souvenir shops and stalls abound in the centre, and there are loads of good photographic opportunities. Please remember to wear modest dress if you do intend going in to the Cathedral – this means that women should cover their shoulders, and neither men nor women should wear shorts. Photography is not permitted if a Mass is in progress.

Perhaps you're a very seasoned cruise traveller, and have not only visited Vigo before, but have also been to Santiago. What else is there to do within reasonable distance of the port? Quite a lot. For example, just 15 miles out of town lies a delightful village that was founded by King Alfonso IX – Bayona La Real. It is more than likely that your cruise line will be offering a tour here as well, and if you've done the City and Santiago before do try this, or again, try a taxi.

Little more than a fishing village, Bayona nonetheless had the distinction of welcoming home Christopher Columbus, one of history's more famous men, from his epic voyage to the New World well over 500 years ago. A replica of one of his ships, the "Pinta" is tied up snugly in the harbour: you can go aboard and wonder at the courage and fortitude of the men who ventured out into the unknown on such a minute and seemingly frail craft. Bayona is called 'La Real' because of its regal connections – 'Royal Bayona' – and the local architecture and ambiance here is exactly as you would expect it to be. The Church of Santa Maria, built in the Ro-man-Gothic style, lies at the village heart and in the adjacent convent the nuns of a cloistered order never see the light of day, although they are commercially astute and produce all sorts of goodies for sale to tourists: make your choice, lay your cash on a revolving table which whisks it away into the gloom within. On the next revolution your souvenir will be delivered to you – all without a word! Bayona is a pretty spot, with glorious beaches and ancient buildings. Visit the fortress of Monte Real – Royal Mountain – which has been successfully commandeered by the local Parador, or state-run hotel. From its genuine ramparts you can enjoy pleasant views of the surrounding countryside and coastline. All in all, I have no hesitation in recommending a visit here, as ithe village itself is pleasant and the journey there and back will take you through some typical Galician scenery.

At the beginning of this chapter I reminded you of the close proximity of the Portuguese border, a matter of only twenty or so miles – and some of you may want to know what this part of Portugal is like. Again I can recom-mend it, for the nearest Portuguese border town – Valença do Minho – is a picturesque and ancient fortified place which offers scenery, antiquity, and lots of opportunities for shopping. Part of the journey from Vigo takes you though less than beautiful industrial sites, but once you're out of town the countryside is rather nice. Not all the cruiselines offer tours here, so you may have to take a taxi – but do remember that it is a forty mile round trip from Vigo port. Hereabouts the border between Spain and Portugal is the River Minho and you'll cross this as you head for your destination. Arrival is a little deceptive as the old and attractive part of Valença is surrounded by a modern, less attractive, one. However, passing through ancient gates you'll find yourselves in a maze of quaint streets, Gothic houses and Romanesque Churches, all surrounded by massive 17th Century walls which were originally built to keep the Spaniards out but which today provide a pleasant blend of history and romance. (You'll also find the odd driver who cares little for your well-being on the narrow streets – do watch out!)

Valença do Minho is one of the nicest places: colourful, bustling little streets, fountains, shady squares, pavement cafes and those shopping opportunities – remember that Portugal is famed for its pottery and linen. Remember, too, that other great product of England's oldest ally – Port wine, which comes in a bewildering selection, all quite delicious. As you might expect, there are lots of good watering holes here, but one of the best, at least in terms of its strategic position, is the local Pousada, or Portuguese State Hotel. Atop a hill, it affords great views across the border into Spain and serves delicious Portuguese snacks to go with the Port or a glass of the famed 'green' wine of the country, 'Vinho Verde'. You certainly won't regret the time taken for this visit.

In summary, then, Vigo has a lot to offer. Stroll the streets of the city itself, visiting its churches, parks, monuments and shops. Sample its wines and enjoy the bustle of a busy, northern Spanish town, where the Galicians are friendly and the seafood delicious. Venture further afield to follow in the footsteps of the myriad pilgrims who have made their journey to the Shrine of St. James and there admire the magnificence of the cathedral which is the very heart of Santiago, or see one of the ships that brought fortune to the coffers of medieval Spain, and wonder at the courage and perseverance of the man who helped to make that fortune a reality, Christopher Columbus. Finally, perhaps, visit Portugal's most northerly outpost at Valence do Minho, perhaps pausing awhile on its massive walls and sipping a glass of chilled white Port.

Whatever you do here, I'm sure you'll enjoy your visit. Then, in the cool of the evening, as your ship sails down the Ria del Vigo towards the restless Atlantic, watch for those rugged inlets, so often battered by the waves that roll endlessly in from America. And enjoy the comfort of your ship, anticipating an excellent dinner after a memorable day in Galicia.

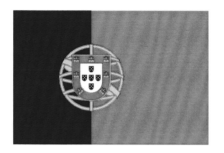

LISBON
Portugal

Bridge of the 25th April

Vasco Da Gama Tower

The Belem Tower

Monument to the Discoveries

Commercial Square

The Cathedral

The National Gallery

LISBON
Cradle of the Navigators

Portugal's capital city is a delight, sitting astride the mighty River Tagus, and one of the best ways to arrive is by sea. Most likely your arrival will be timed for around 8am, and if it is then its worth being up and about and on deck, for you'll be rewarded with the sight of the sun rising behind Lisbon's magnificent 'Bridge of the 25th April', modelled on San Francisco's Golden Gate, and built by the same engineers.

Lisbon has been a great city for centuries: the Phoenicians occupied the area in around 1200 BC and the Romans were here at the end of the 1st Century BC: but it started to gain recognition under the Moors from the 8th - 12th Centuries AD and became even more important when the Ottoman Turks seized Constantinople in 1453.

Columbus came here to live, and it was in Lisbon that he nurtured many of his dreams and plans. But Portugal's home-grown Prince Henry, the Infante Dom Henrique, did much to put Lisbon on the world's map. He laid the foundation for Portugal's massive sea borne trading empire which reached its peak in the late 15th and early 16th centuries.

Sailing up the Tagus river, just before reaching the bridge, you'll see on your left hand the tower that a proud King Manuel I built as a place from which to welcome home his triumphant sailors. The Torre de Belém is a fine example of Manueline architecture.

Behind it, set back from the riverside, stands the Jerónimos Monastery, one of the very few survivors of a devastating earthquake that cost 40,000 lives and all but destroyed the city in 1755. Inside lie the remains of Vasco Da Gama, arguably Portugal's greatest sailor who found the way to the east in 1498, succeeding where Columbus failed. Most people know of him – novice sailors are often nicknamed 'Vasco' – but I thought it might be interesting to dwell for a few minutes on his life and that of some of his predecessors because their voyages are the very fabric of the history of Lisbon. Since they are so important to our story, it is appropriate to try to find out what motivated them and what prompted Prince Henry to forgo his life at Court with all the privileges that were his as Prince of Portugal in favour of a more precarious existence by far. What made his captains take their lives in their hands in a pursuit that could at best be described as rather dubious?

I don't profess to be an historian, but it seems to me that a brief look at this history is important.

The fall of Constantinople to the Ottoman Turks in 1453 placed the silk road, hitherto the main artery from which the west imported the goods of the East in the hands of Islam, creating for the West a desperate need to find another route which would ensure continuity of supply of those Oriental necessities – and necessities they were: spices masked the unpleasantness of un-refrigerated meat and perfumes hid the smell of unwashed bodies.The Crusaders had introduced Europeans to these commodities and the demand was insatiable; but the Crusades had failed in their principal objective which was to over-run a militant Islam: Christendom simply did not have the wherewithal to oust the Muslims from the eastern and southern shores of the Mediterranean where they had become so firmly ensconced, and after the fall of Constantinople the desired riches of the East could only be had on terms dictated by them.

By the 1300s, most western Europeans had grown weary of fighting the Moors, and only in the Iberian Peninsular was the crusading spirit still very much alive. There, the three Christian kingdoms of Castile, Aragon and Portugal recognised that the Muslims would never willingly release heir hold on east-west trade and, all three, being seafaring nations, might have been expected to pursue an alternative trade route.

But Aragon's coastline was Mediterranean, and it seemed that she wished to limit her horizons to that sea at that time; Castile, although facing both the Atlantic and the Mediterranean, found herself too busy defending her southern border against Granada, the last Moorish outpost on the peninsular and had neither the time nor the resources to fund exploration. So, it fell to little Portugal to do all the running. In the 1300s Portugal had a population of less than a million, but nevertheless she possessed a viable, growing number of merchant vessels trading on the sea routes to France, England and Flanders.

Isolated from the Mediterranean and facing into the Atlantic, Portugal was ideally situated for oceanic adventure with prevailing winds off her coast most suitable for south and south-westward exploration. They say that if you stand at the end of Europe on Cape St. Vincent you'll hear the call of distant lands in the pounding of the Atlantic rollers at the foot of the massive cliffs you'll find there: maybe it was this call that first motivated Prince Henry, the third son of King John I and his wife, Phillipa, daughter of John of Gaunt. With his brothers Edward and Peter, Henry took part in an attack on Ceuta, the Spanish enclave in Morocco which stands on the opposite side of the Straits from the Rock of Gibraltar. During this expedition, Henry realised the importance of seapower and became aware of the fact that the Muslim Empire extended a considerable way down the west coast of Africa. He reasoned that, if he could get Portuguese ships to remain at sea long enough, he could strike a blow for Christendom by attacking the Muslims at their weakest point – at the extremity of their empire. Here Medieval mythology played a role in Henry's plans: it was a popular belief that remote pockets of Christianity existed throughout the Muslim world, and tales abound of Henry's ships crusading against the Moors, forging down the coast of Africa with the red cross of Christ emblazoned on their sails, their men intent upon joining up eventually with the mighty Christian armies of legendary Priest-King Prester John before going on to outflank Islam and to reconquer Jerusalem. Commercially astute, Henry now had a foundation upon which he could develop other, rather more secular, ideals – religious fervour.

He gave up court life and moved to Lagos on modern Portugal's Algarve, there to pursue his study of mathematics, astronomy and geography. At the extreme south western tip of Portugal he built a fortress, naval arsenal, small town and school of navigation at Sagres, and it was here that his pilots received their training and commissions. Between 1444 and 1446 he sanctioned more than 30 voyages to Guinea, and set up a prototype fortified trading post at Arguin Island, from where he shipped thousands of black slaves back to work the under-populated fields of home.

Henry died in 1460 long before the fulfilment of his vision, and Portuguese oceanic exploration only began in earnest during the reign of John II, who ruled between 1481 and 1495. John enlarged on Henry's vision and took major steps to implement it, and it was he who sent a courtier called Diogo Cao southward along the coast of Africa where in due course he discovered the mouth of the Congo. It was John who championed the Pioneers who did so much to build his little country's astonishing empire – household names such as Bartolomeu Dias, Vasco Da Gama, Pedro Álvares Cabral, Afonso de Albuquerque and others less well known but no less brave – men who made Portuguese the 'Lingua Franca' all around the Indian Ocean rim, eastward through the Indonesian archipelago and northward from the Straits of Malacca to Japan. For a century and more these men held in their hands the rich, seaborne trade of the East – what a trade it was and what an empire it produced! How did its capital city develop?

To answer that, let us now return to the present, and our passage up the mighty Tagus.

Just beyond the Belêm Tower you'll see the striking Monument to the Discoveries, built in its present form in the 1960s to commemorate the feats of the extraordinary men about whom I've been speaking – the navigators who created the empire and extended Portugal's horizons so dramatically. By now the magnificence of the enormous bridge that spans the river just ahead is almost upon you – the Bridge of the 25th April, which was named to commemorate the day in 1974 when the dictator Caetano was deposed in a bloodless coup which ushered in the present day Democratic Republic of Portugal. Approaching the bridge you'll be convinced that the mast and funnel of your ship are going to hit its roadway but, miracle of miracles, you will pass safely underneath, well clear of the structure soaring above.

The bridge has a honeycomb steel roadbed, and the roar of traffic passing overhead emits the sound of a gigantic swarm of bees! On the opposite, right hand, bank of the river looms the magnificent Statue of Christ the Redeemer, 752 feet high and paid for after World War II by Lisbon's womenhood, grateful for Portugal's neutrality and the fact that their husbands and sons were never at risk in that conflict. Many of you will be familiar with Rio de Janiero and will recognise the similarity that this statue has to the famous one that overlooks that city, and will be reminded of the close relationship between the two places.

Having passed beneath the bridge you'll see a number of quays all along the riverbank on your left. Larger ships will probably use the one nearest the bridge which is called Alcântara, whilst smaller ones sometimes berth further up the river. But, wherever you berth it is quite a long walk to town, and the probability is that your cruise line will provide you with a complimentary shuttle service, either to Rossio Square or to Commercial Square, both of which are near the heart of the city. You'll also find an excellent tram service running parallel with the river just outside the dock gates.

To begin your tour of the city, imagine for a few minutes that you want to wander about at your own pace and see some of the things that are to be seen within reasonable walking distance of the centre. I've already said that the cruise berths are, for the most part, a little too far to walk unless you are really determined, so let's assume that you'll either take the shuttle provided, or take a tram for your journey to the centre.

Your aim is to get to Rossio, the Piccadilly Circus of Lisbon (real name Praca Dom Pedro IV). On your way there you'll pass one of Lisbon's more famous squares, almost universally (and wrongly) called 'Black Horse Square' by visiting cruiseship passengers. Don't ask a native to direct you to Black Horse Square, because he will not have heard of it! The square got its 'nickname' from the massive statue of Dom Jose atop his horse that dominates it. Actually, it would be more appropriately named 'Green Horse Square', because of the verdigris which today covers the whole of the monument. The square's real name is Praça do Comércio and it is a huge area, bounded on three sides by colonnaded buildings and on the fourth by the Tagus waterfront. If your shuttle bus is destined to drop you off here, you may find it useful to know that there is a Tourist Information Office at the landward end of the square, on the left hand side when looking

at the triumphal arch and there is an internet café inside the office for those itching to get at their e-mails. Commercial Square is the terminus for many of the city's Tourist Trams and Buses, and these offer a good and inexpensive way of seeing the central sights.
The landward side of the square is dominated by a magnificent triumphal arch spanning the Rua Augusta, heart of the Baixa, or central district that lies in the shadow of the hilltop home of the Castle of St. George.

Baixa is a grid of bustling streets, fine shops, pavement cafes and flower kiosks and Rua Augusta, its principal artery, is pedestrianised from end to end and really comes alive at about ten thirty in the morning when crowds throng beneath the arch from Commercio, heading to town.

At the landward end of Rua Augusta stands Rossio Square, northwestwards of which is Restauradores and the foot of the magnificent Avenida da Liberdade, home to banks, the finest hotels and the main Tourist Information Office. At the farthest end of the Avenida stands the statue of the Marquis de Pombal, the man who was responsible for designing and rebuilding the city following the 1755 earthquake.

In Rossio Square itself a statue of Dom Pedro IV tops a tall pedestal and if you stand beneath it in its shadow and look south towards the river whence you've come, you'll have towering high on your left the Castle of St. George with the old quarter called Alfama tumbling down the hillside beneath, and on your right the Bairro Alto, or high town, crowned by the ruined Carmel Convent whose roof fell in onto the congregation that fateful day of earthquake. In the heart of Baixa a block or two in front of you there is a lift called the Elevator of Santa Justa (built in 1902 by an engineer called Raull Mesnier) and this will take you up to the Convent for a couple of Euros – you'll find the ride up well worth it for there is a little café at the top where the view down over Baixa is rewarding. From this vantage point, look across the 'valley' of the central district to the opposite hillside where stands the Castle of St. George, the views from which are stunning

From here look across the river to that magnificent statue of Christ the Redeemer far away on the southern shore. The twisting, ancient streets and buildings of the Alfama clutter the hillside below you: this is the oldest part of the city and quite a bit of it survived the devastation of the earthquake. Alfama really gives you the flavour of Old Lisbon, and with a little imagination you can see Da Gama and his sailors wending their way through the narrow streets to the ships waiting patiently on the nearby waterfront.
In the heart of Alfama stands Lisbon's Romanesque Cathedral, called "The Se", its twin towers framing great rose window. The once beautiful embellishments of King John V were swept away by the earthquake and restorers who followed it, leaving an interior that today is verging on the drab. In

all, I find the cathedral rather austere – a Gothic pile with a Romanesque façade. Nevertheless it is a commanding presence in the profusion of Alfama's ancient streets.

Let us now take a closer look at some of the sights we've touched on, and then expand our horizons a little. Starting on the waterfront, a short distance eastward of the berth at Alcantara you can't miss the towering masts and spars of the 19th century frigate *"Dom Fernando Due e Gloria"*, today a well preserved ship and floating museum. At one time in the distant past she sank in the Tagus, was discovered, refloated and restored, and became an important exhibit in the International Exposition of 1998, about which a little more later. For you lovers of things nautical, she is a must!

If you want to ride a local train, you can board one at Alcantara station just outside the dock gate, and two or three stops eastward you'll reach Cais do Sodra, which is well within walking distance of Black Horse Square. Ride the same train in the opposite direction and it'll take you all the way downriver to Cascais: from the train you can enjoy lovely views along the coast for most of the hour long journey, en route passing through the district of Belem. At this point in our discussion we'll leave the train for a time and talk about this delightful area of the city.

Belém Station stands close to that proud memorial to Henry and his captains, the stylised concrete caravel with its prow adorned by statues of the navigators, the Monument to the Discoveries. You can take a lift to the top of the monument and look down at the mosaic of the Portuguese Empire which lies on the pavement beneath – that Empire discussed at the very beginning of this chapter, initiated by Prince Henry and created by so many of the captains who sailed in his wake.

Across the busy main road – and it really is busy so please don't attempt to cross it other than via the underpass thoughtfully provided – stands Jerónimos Monastery, wondrous testament to the Manueline architectural style and another earthquake survivor. Inside you'll see the tomb of Da Gama who died in 1524 and at that of his patron, King Manuel.

The west wing of the monastery is home to Lisbon's mammoth Maritime Museum, one of the finest of its type that I know.

Nearby is the Coach Museum, also well worth a visit. One of its oldest exhibits dates from the 16th century, and many of the gilded masterpieces on show date back to the early 18th century, legacy from a regal age.

Then, of course, in the very same vicinity is the Belém Tower, or Torre de

Belèm, which has come to symbolise the city, used as it is in many a tourist brochure. Manueline in style, Torre de Belem was commissioned by King Manuel in the early 1500s and stood originally on an island in the stream of the Tagus. Today, the waters have been diverted so that it now graces the foreshore. It is surrounded by a pleasant, shady park wherein stands a life-sized monument of a seaplane, commemorating the first flight from Lisbon to Brazil: the original aircraft may be seen in the aviation section of the Maritime Museum.

This whole area is a delight, with attractive cafes, bistros and restaurants, boutiques and craft shops galore. The local marina with its many yachts testifies to Portugal's maritime past and speaks of the popularity of this area, for the owners of expensive yachts always seem to gravitate to the best parts of seafront towns! As I've said, you can go on from here on your train journey, eventually ending up in Cascais. But I'm not going to take you there just yet.

In the city, lovers of churches may want to visit the Basilica A Estrella, whose massive dome is another of Lisbon's better known landmarks. Built in the 18th century by a grateful Queen Maria who made a promise to God that, if he granted her a son, she would build him a church. She had her son, honoured her promise, and the church stands testament to her devotion. Or, you may wish to visit the Church of Santa Engracia, or The Se, which I've already described.

Back once more in our now familiar Rossio Square you'll find the unmistakable bulk of the National Theatre standing on the northern perimeter.This was built in the 1840s on the site of a former Palace of Inquisitions, in front of which public hangings were carried out, convicted heretics were burned at the stake and sundry other unspeakable acts performed. Today, the Theatre presides over a more peaceful scene, although the bus station which occupies one side of the square gets a little hectic at times!

The imposing frontage of Rossio Railway Station marks the start of Restauradores and the foot of the Avenida da Liberdade, that massive multi lane highway that strikes northwest from this part of town. Just beyond the railway station, heading up the Avenida and on the left you'll find the Tourist Information Office next door to a fine theatre built in the Art Deco style. Walk the length of the Avenida to the square where stands that monument to the Marquis de Pombal, perched atop his pedestal gazing down over his re-designed and rebuilt city which nestles between his lofty perch and the glimmering waters of the Tagus flowing serenely to the sea in the middle distance. Here too you'll find the green serenity Edward VII Park, named after our own King who visited Lisbon in 1903. In the park stand two notable buildings: one is called Estufa Quente, a huge hot house full of exotic plants and lush foliage, and the other Estufa Fria, a corresponding cold house which is a venue for periodic antiques fairs, classical concerts and other similar extravaganzas.

The National Museum, or Foundation Calouste Gulbenkian, is the city's principal cultural centre and is not to be missed. Standing just to the north of Edward VII Park, the Foundation opened its doors in 1969 and features Classical, Oriental and European Art sections, where masterpieces by Ghirlandaio, Rubens, Rembrandt, Van Dyck, Gainsborough, Turner and Lawrance can be seen alongside the impressionist works of Monet, Degas and Manet. Chinese ceramics, Japanese lacqueurware and furniture from the reigns of Louis XV and Louis XIV along with the crystal of Renè Lalique ensure that there is something of interest for everyone.

Next to Rossio is a another imposing square, the Praça da Figuera where from his statue, King John I gazes down on his subjects hurrying hither and thither at his feet. Figuera, too, lies in the shadow of St George, and earlier I said that his castle is worth visiting. Take a bus, or a taxi, or if you want to get the full flavour of the Alfama, walk. (You can, of course, take transport up and walk down – much easier on the legs!) Nearing the top you'll be rewarded with ever widening vistas over the city and its river. The castle was built originally during the period of Moorish domination, and is well preserved. It has peaceful, shady grounds and turreted parapets from which to admire the views spread beneath. Up here, artists paint and ply their wares, as do craft people of all types, and there is a pleasant, tranquil, atmosphere: the views over Baixa and the Tagus are spectacular.

You old soldiers and lovers of things military will like to know that on the waterfront southeast of the Castle stands another regional railway station, Santa Apolonia, notable because the Museo Militar (Military Museum) stands adjacent. This boasts a good collection of cannons, unusual firearms, military documents and suchlike, the whole housed in a building with an impressive Corinthian façade.

Ceramic tiles, especially blue and white ones, are universally regarded as a symbol of Portugal. Called Azulejo, they will be found almost everywhere in Lisbon – inside, outside, on monuments, shops, benches and in parks. But one of the best places to see them is in the Museum dedicated to them, the 'Museu Nacional do Azulejo' which lies further eastwards still from the Military Museum. Here you can trace their development and see countless examples as well as the longest one ever produced, a panorama of Lisbon that measures about 120 feet in length!

Lisbon was host to Expo '98 and 'The Park of Nations' is the site that was developed especially for that international event. Three and half miles upriver to the east from the city, it offers a variety of attractions ranging from an Oceanarium, said to be the second largest in the world, to various educational exhibits all spread over a massive, pedestrianised area with a profusion of restaurants, cafes, pavilions and fountains. The Vasco Da Gama Tower offers spectacular views across the Tagus at this, one of its widest points and from it you can gaze at the recently completed, 12 mile long bridge that is also named after the famous seaman. In the Park you'll find a diversity of shopping opportunities and, if it's all too much for your legs, you can view it from the airy comfort of a cable car that spans the site.

I hope that in this overview I've managed to convey some of the flavour of this city for you. It is a real delight to me – I love the place, and hope that I've been able to give you a glimpse that will lead you to want to explore it for yourselves.

Many of you will sample the tours on offer, and the likelihood is that they've been well described for you by the on-board Tours Manager or Port Lecturer, so I'm not going to dwell at length on those, and after all this book is really aimed at the independent visitor. But I will touch on one or two in order to give the reader a flavour of what is likley to be on offer.

There will be a 'Lisbon Highlights Tour', or similar, which will enable you to see most of the things so far discussed from the comfort of a coach. You'll probably visit Belèm and the Coach and Maritime Museums, and likely go on through the residential suburb of Restelo, arriving back at the centre by way of Pombal's statue, the Avenida da Liberdade and Rossio Square.
Then there will be a tour visiting Sintra and Cascais and if you've been to Lisbon before but now want to enjoy some of its delightful surroundings, this is the one for you because Sintra is a pretty little place which was described by Lord Byron as a 'Glorious Eden'. The Royal Palace dominates the village – note especially the strange, conical chimneys reminiscent of the Oast Houses of Kent. One time summer residence of Portugal's kings and the Moorish lords before them, the Palace owes its design to the Moors, and it was they who built the fortress that stands atop the hillside above the town, the Castelo dos Mouro. A stop in the central square gives you a chance to have a coffee in one of the delightful cafes before strolling and browsing amongst the many shops and boutiques that abound. There is a little Regional Museum just off the main square, and one of its central exhibits is a model of the Royal Palace. After Sintra your coach will probably take you to Cabo da Roca, mainland Europe's westernmost point. If it stops at the viewpoint you'll have the chance to photograph the rugged headland and listen to the Atlantic's pounding waves far beneath. Your coach will continue southwards for Cascais, popular beach resort of the Portuguese Riviera. Cascais has enjoyed the patronage of Europe's royalty and aristocracy for generations: today, its elegant houses, modern

marina, pretty waterfont and town centre entice visitors from every walk of life and in the height of the season it becomes very crowded. Numerous bars and cafes stand ready to slake your thirst and ease those pangs of hunger – after all, it's been sometime since breakfast! The Citadel on the waterfront frames the Praia da Ribeira, where traditional fishing boats lie drawn up on the tideline. Leaving Cascais, you'll return to Lisbon by way of Estoril, a town of luxury hotels, golf courses, Lisbon's largest Casino and excellent beaches. Your journey home from here runs all along the northern shore of the river, passing Belêm once more before arriving at the docks and your waiting ship.

I started this chapter with a discussion about Henry the Navigator, and I talked of Bartolomeu Dias who first rounded that far-off headland which is today called the Cape of Good Hope; I looked at Vasco Da Gama, whose name has cropped up throughout the chapter because he was, after all, the man who found the sea road to the east. These men were not, by any means, the only seafarers who helped their nation to carve for itself such a deep niche in oceanic history. I could have spoken of Francis Xavier, so called second apostle of the Indies, so active in those lands with his ministry taking him from East Africa to India, around the Bay of Bengal to Malacca and Indonesia, thence to Kagoshima in Japan, but this is not the place to do so. But what of today, you may ask? Where is that Empire now? Some 163 years after Henry the Navigator, King Sebastian died with his army at Ksar El Kebir in Morocco, and this led to the takeover of his kingdom by Philip II of Spain, and to 60 years of 'Spanish Capitivity' that sapped Portugal's manpower and led to much of its empire being snatched by the Dutch and the English, traditional enemies of Imperial Spain. Even so, vestiges of her empire remained some right up to our day. For example, Goa, last remnant of Da Gama's and Albuquerque's Portuguese India, held out until 1961, and Portugal only ceded independence to Mocambique and Angola in the 1970s: Macau reverted to China in 1999, two years after Hong Kong. Where did it all go? Perhaps in answer we could look at the words of a Portuguese diplomat who once remarked that his country should feature in the "Guinness Book of Records" as possessing the worst businessmen on earth, for he said, and I quote:
"We had a one hundred year grip on the world's richest trade, and ended up poorer. We let the wealth of the east slip through our fingers into the coffers of Antwerp's merchant syndicates, and proceeds were lavished on Moroccan wars, dynastic marriages and ostentatious display."
So, whilst the Empire no longer exists, the legacy left by the Portuguese Navigators for a certainty remains – they achieved a lasting geographic revolution if not a financial one: by and large they interacted successfully with ancient cultures, and gave humanity the vision of the single world.
For all of them, their home was Lisbon a beautiful, vibrant and historic city.

CADIZ
Spain

Theatre (Gran Teatro Falla)

Monument to the Constitution

Plaza San Juan de Dios

Dragon Tree

Old Tobacco Factory

Cathedral

Customs House

CADIZ
Europe's oldest city?

Spain and Portugal share the Iberian peninsular, although Spain is, of course, the dominant occupant. The peninsular has a very long history indeed and its oldest historical findings date back to something like 30,000 BC – far too long ago for us to be worried about, although the archaeologists among you may know that the most important remains of this period will be found at the caves of Cova Negra and Pinar, near Granada.

Leaving pre-history aside, the first tribes to take up residence probably came from North Africa and they founded an important settlement in the valley of the Guadalquivir river, down in the south. But the North Africans were not to enjoy their exclusive occupancy for long: in around 1200 BC Celtic tribes from the north infiltrated their domain, co-habited, and so created the Celt-Iberian race.

Then, in about 1000 BC the Phoenicians arrived and started to establish colonies, the most important of which was called Gadir, today's Cadiz. Next came the Carthaginians, who invaded and conquered large areas of the peninsular and established communities in many parts, the most important of which were in Ibiza and Cartagena, the 'new' Carthage.
The Punic Wars of the third century AD established Rome's supremacy in the Western Mediterranean, and Roman armies conquered the entire peninsular creating the Roman province of Hispania which was to become significantly important to the Empire in many ways, not least of which the fact that no less than two Emperors hailed from here – Trajan and Hadrian.

Declining Roman power in the fifth century saw Gothic tribes flooding in and establishing a kingdom in 419AD and their domination lasted until 711AD when again North African incomers crossed the Straits of Gibraltar.

The Muslim armies defeated Roderic, the last Visigoth king, and began to establish a Moorish domination which was to prevail for around seven hundred years. Moorish architectural influences can be clearly seen almost everywhere, from the palaces of the Alhambra to the markets of Malaga. By and large, the country prospered under Arab rule, especially in the south which became known as 'al-Andalus' (corrupted to Andalucia), where new agricultural techniques and sciences brought new-found wealth. But, as always seems to be the way, the peace and prosperity did not last. Pockets of Christian resistance in the north of the country were boosted by the squabbles which broke out amongst the ruling noble families of the south, enabling relatively minor insurrections to blossom into a a war which lasted for seven hundred years – the "Reconquista" – one which was ended finally on January 2nd 1492, when the Moors under

Boabdil surrendered Granada to the Catholic Monarchs, Ferdinand of Aragon and Isabela of Castile.

Military conflict over, it wasn't long before an ideological one began and Ferdinand and Isabela, having managed to unite the vast country under their joint crown, set about a radical clean-up and spared no effort in their quest to re-Christianise the populace – whether the populace wanted to be Christians or not. First, Jews who refused to be baptised Christians were expelled. They were followed in short order by dissenting Muslims and it wasn't long before the whole of Spain became engulfed in a crusade which became one of the most infamous in history – the Spanish Inquisition.

In the meantime Columbus, Genoese adventurer and man of huge persuasion and resolution, secured for himself the backing of the Catholic Monarchs, assembled a fleet and sailed westward into the history books when he crossed the "Sea of Darkness" and made a landfall in San Salvador – Columbus had 'found' America (note that I did not say he discovered it – that is another story, and not one for this book). Discover it or not, his exploits nonetheless brought for his sponsors untold and undreamed of wealth, and the gold and silver that flowed from the New World into the coffers of Spain made her one of the most powerful nations on earth in the era that came to be known as her "Golden Age" – and much of that wealth flowed in through Cadiz.

Isabela died in 1504 and her daughter Joan, who was married to the German Emperor's son Philip, succeeded her to the throne. This marriage led to unity with the Hapsburgs and an era of considerable power and prosperity which only ended with the defeat of the Spanish Armada in 1588.

Charles II, the last Hapsburg king, died without descendant, and Philip of Bourbon, nephew of Louis XIV of France, ascended the throne. Then came the French Revolution – Spain declared war on the new republic but lost and Napoleon set his brother Joseph on the Spanish throne, much to the fury of the Spaniards who fought for their independence for five years.

After Napoleon's defeat at Waterloo in 1815, King Ferdinand VII took the throne and ruled with an iron rod. He changed the law of succession so that his daughter Isabel could be Queen, but his brother Charles rebelled and started the Seven Years War which led to economic and political chaos, culminating in the revolution of 1868 and the formation of the so-called First Republic. But even this didn't last – Isabela's son Alfonso XII restored the kingdom in a coup d'etat in 1878. A disastrous war with the United States in 1895 led to the loss of Spain's last overseas possession, Cuba, and a deepening economic crises which took Spain to the brink of civil war and led to the establishment of a military dictatorship.

In the elections of 1931 the political Left triumphed and the King was forced to leave the country. Internal conflict led to the Spanish Civil war of 1936-1939 when the Nationalists of General Franco received extensive support from Nazi Germany and gained victory over the Republicans. Franco kept Spain neutral during World War II, a decision that led to political and economic isolation and a long period of stagnation.

During the 1950s and 60s stringent efforts were made to restore international relations, the economy recovered and in 1969 Franco declared Juan Carlos de Bourbon to be his successor, with the title of king. When Franco died in 1975, a constitutional monarchy was established.

So, to bring us up to date, Spain became a member of NATO in 1985, joined the European community in 1986, hosted the Olympic Games in Barcelona in 1992, and staged the World Exposition EXPO '92 in Seville, when Madrid was declared European Cultural Capital.

So Spain has a long, varied and sometimes bloody history and Cadiz, its southernmost city, claims to be the oldest in all of Europe. The city and its near neighbor San Fernando are in fact sited on an island separated from the mainland by a series of flood channels but connected to it by a several bridges, the whole creating a massive bay which proved large enough to accommodate the combined fleets of Admirals Villeneuve and Gravina immediately before they were engaged by Nelson, just up the coast off Cape Trafalgar, on that fateful day in October 1805.

Cadiz occupies the southernmost tip of the island, and the whole of the oldest part of it is surrounded by the fortifications of King Alfonso X. In all likelihood, your ship will berth in the Puerto Commercial, which is really very close to the centre of the old town.

The Plaza de Espana, very close to the dock gates, which is home to the Monument to the Spanish Constitution, is separated by a length of waterfront from the Plaza San Juan de Dios where stands the City Hall. A very short distance to the south of the square is the city's most important building, the Cathedral. Built in the Neo-Classical style between the 18th and 19th centuries, it has two aisles and several side chapels. The choir stalls are worthy of note as they originated in an old Carthusian monastery and the adjacent Cathedral Museum has a fine collection of artefacts, ivory carvings, and other works of art.

The city fathers created an almost unique tourist-aid when they decided to paint a coloured line on the pavement to guide visitors to all the most interesting sites. Depending on the season, this sometimes disappears until someone re-paints it, but if found intact, it is invaluable because all you have to do is follow it! Called, appropriately, the 'Tourist Walk' it starts at the Plaza de Espana, passes the Museum of Cadiz which has both Fine Arts and Archaeological sections, takes in the Church of San Felipe Neri where a painting of the Immaculate Conception by Murillo dominates the high altar, then turns eastwards shortly after this heading for the next attraction on the route, the Torre Tavira. Climb this to the viewing platform at the top, and enjoy an excellent view over the old town. Tavira also houses a Camera Obscura, which will interest the photographers amongst you.

Still heading eastwards, pass by another church called Iglesia de Santa Maria, then you'll reach the Cathedral that I've told you about: get there and you're now just a hop, skip and a jump from the Plaza San Juan de Dios, where a Tourist Information Office is located at its western end.

The Plaza is a pleasant shady area, almost completely surrounded by restaurants and pavement cafes. The coloured line route does not cover the whole of Old Cadiz and for some of the other sites of interest you'll have to deviate from it. On the northern waterfront enjoying superb views across the harbour mouth is a pleasant garden called Alameda Apodaca – look for the trees here, for they have amazing branches sweeping down almost to the pavement, their massive boughs luxuriant with enormous leaves that provide welcome relief at the height of the noonday sun. At this point, Alfonso's fortifications form a seafront parapet illuminated at night by massive lanterns that seem to hail from a bygone age. Look out across the Bay of Cadiz from here, and it's not hard to picture those galleons sailing in laden with treasures from the New World, and easy to imagine the combined armadas of France and Spain assembling before Trafalgar. It is a most attractive spot.

On the western seafront is another garden called Parque Genoves, near to a very significant part of the fortifications, the Castillo Santa Catalina, jutting belligerently into the sea, albeit that its defensive cannons have been silent a long time. Beyond the fortress is one of the local beaches, the Playa de la Caleta, but this is not the most convenient one for the ship: there is a better beach beyond the Cathedral, much closer to the docks.

Leave the Parque Genoves behind you and head back into town and you'll come upon a fine theatre, the Gran Teatro Falla. In this area especially, the old city is a wealth of narrow streets, pleasing courtyards, bustling plazas and churches, some of which I've not yet mentioned. Among them are the Church of Santa Cueva, which features frescoes by Goya; the church of San Augustin, which boasts carvings by Martinez Montanes, and the church of San Francisco. Also worth seeing is the Hospital des Mujeres which has Baroque bell-gables and a beautiful patio sporting a painting by El Greco called the "Stigmatization of St. Francis of Assisi". Today, this is the Bishop's Palace.

At the landward end of the peninsular and separating the old city from the new you'll pass through a set of ancient city gates, the Murallas de Cadiz. Nearby is the old Tobacco Factory, today defunct in that role but resurrected as a modern Conference Centre and grandly re-named the Palace of Congress.

Thus ends your tour of the old city. There is a new one, of course, which runs the length of the peninsular towards San Fernando, but it is not very exciting and there is more than enough, I promise you, to keep you occupied in the old – unless you are a serious shopper, in which case you'll need to know that shopping opportunities are a little limited in the old town. Small boutiques, gift shops and corner shops for the residents are really the order of the day here although there is a bustling market very close to the main post office which stands in a square called Plaza de la Flores. But if you want bigger shops, you'll have to visit the new town and then my advice would be to take a taxi.

Just outside the dock gates on the adjacent road which is called, predictably, the Avenida del Puerto, you can pick up an open-topped Tourist Bus and from this see everything that I've described (and no doubt lots more!) without having to walk: again, this is a good, inexpensive way to see the sights. Old Cadiz is really quite small, the going is flat, and a walk from end to end is not a major expedition. But you may wish to venture further afield, in which case your cruise line will undoubtedly have a number of tours on offer and again, it would be remiss of me not to outline some of these.

One may take you to Seville, but, being another major town, it falls outside the scope of this chapter. All I'll say is that Seville is beautiful, very historic, with a Cathedral of mammoth proportions wherein Seville's city fathers insist lie the bones of Columbus, interred in a monumental tomb: whether he really is in there has been the subject of debate for many years, as other cities in Spain and elsewhere, lay claim to being his final resting place.

Almost certainly you'll be offered a tour to Jerez de la Frontera, the heart of the local winelands and home to Sherry, celebrated and renowned product of this region. Take this tour and you're likely to be away from your ship for five or six hours, for Jerez lies some miles inland and your tour of a wine 'Bodegas' will take a little time. Leaving the quayside, you'll drive past the old Tobacco Factory and through the Murallas Gates before traversing the length of the new town. Just before San Fernando, you'll swing sharp left and cross the bridge which takes you over the estuary, past the shipyards which are still active and provide employment for many from these parts. This sprawling industrial area soon gives way to the pleasant rolling countryside of Andalucia. The drive to Jerez takes a little under an hour and as you get nearer to the town you'll start to pass through the vineyards which have made the region so famous. Jerez is a thriving town and one of the best known in southern Spain because of its association with the famous wine that bears its name. Several 'Bodegas' are located here, but you'll likely visit that of Gonzalez Byas, known worldwide for its evocative 'Tio Pepe' logo. Your tour will take you through every part of the winery, the production process will be described to you in great detail, and will culminate in a wine tasting when you'll have a chance to sample sherry in all its delightful and many guises. The Guinness Book of Records says that the 'Tio Pepe' weather vane, which soars over one of the Bodegas' warehouses, is the largest in the world, and looking at it, you can understand why! Before re-boarding your coach you'll be taken to the on-site shop where for a very few Euros you can buy a bottle or two to take back to the ship, there to enjoy at leisure (ship's rules permitting!)

Sometimes the tour to Jerez includes a visit to the world famous Royal Andalucian Equestrian School: if yours does, then you'll enjoy the sight of magnificent Andalucian horses performing in a show which has got to be one of the most spectacular of all equestrian events, then, after the performance you'll be shown around the stables and the stalls that make up the rest of the complex.
Afterwards, your drive back to Cadiz is pleasant and relaxing, giving you time to reflect on all the things you've seen (or sleep off the effects of some of the things you've tasted!)

Another tour may take you to the 'White Villages of Andalucia', a journey into the heartland of old Spain which will bring to life some of my earlier discussion of the country's history. One of the places likely to be on the agenda is Medina Sidonia, an excellent example of an unspoilt Spanish Village with little cobbled streets, red-tiled white buildings, Gothic Church and Moorish gate. From here you'll probably drive on to Arcos de la Frontera, which, by virtue of its quaint beauty, has been declared a national historic monument.

Do remember the advice I've given you before: if planning to go into some of the beautiful churches that I've described, please observe the dress code – no bare shoulders, and no shorts. Don't carry unnecessary valuables or cash with you, for opportunists are everywhere, even in smaller cities like Cadiz. As you sail out in the evening, look out over the port side of your ship just after clearing the harbour breakwater and you'll see those ancient lanterns lining Alfonso's waterfront and, if the timing is right, you'll see them twinkling into life and garlanding the ancient waterfront, leaving you with memories that will make you glad that you came!

MALAGA
Spain

Paseo del Parque

The Cathedral

Gibralfaro Castle

Picasso's House

The Bullring

Town Hall

Harbour view

MALAGA
From Pablo Picasso to a Myriad of Tourists

The capital of the Costa del Sol, Malaga is one of the most popular destinations in all of Spain. It is also the most important of all the coastal cities
of Andalucia, and is, in fact, a typical Andaluz place with a fierce individual-
ism that has been largely untouched by tourism and the passage of time.
But it does seem that it has always attracted visitors, for there was an established population here when the Phoenicians first arrived from Tyre,
some 50 years after Troy was destroyed in 1184 BC. It was they who
named the place 'Malaca' possibly after their word for salt – Malac – for
this was, for them, an important fish-salting centre. Or maybe they named
it after their word for "Queen", 'Malaka': we shall probably never know.

There are two fortresses overlooking the city – the higher is called Gibralfaro, the lower, Alcazaba. The Alcazaba is Phoenician in origin, doubtless
the building of which symbolised their determination to stay. They successfully left their mark here in other ways as well, for there are several Phoenician artefacts to be seen in the local archaeological museum.

The Greeks followed the Phoenicians and they, in turn, were followed by
the Romans, who colonised this part of Spain in around 218BC and stayed
on for about six hundred years. They enlarged the Alcazaba fortress, and
then built a theatre at its base. This has been partially excavated and is
open to the public – although it must be said that it always seems to be the
subject of more digging and is, more often than not, closed and festooned
with scaffolding.

As we saw in the last chapter, Spain as a whole suffered invasion at the
hands of the Moors in 711 AD, and it was the Moors who named this region Al-Andalus, corrupted in our day to Andalucia. Malaga became a major Moorish city, and you can see that culture's influence all over the place
and especially in the Alcazaba fortress, which they enlarged, using mate-
rial filched from the Roman Theatre.
Malaga remained Moorish for over 700 years, and was, in fact, one of the
last Moorish strongholds on the Iberian peninsular to fall to the Catholic
monarchs Isabela and Ferdinand, in 1487.

Your ship will berth in the Commercial Harbour, the precise berth depend-
ant upon the size of the ship. Of necessity, larger ships will berth further
out, smaller ships closer in. If you're on one of the larger ones and lie further out, then your cruise line will probably provide a free shuttle service
from the quayside to the dock gates: if you're on a smaller ship, then such
a service should not be necessary, for you're likely to tie up almost in the

city centre. Either way, the gateway to the town is the Plaza de la Marina, a large and busy square just outside the port. This is a good reference point – think of it as the centre of a clock, and imagine you're standing there, looking northwards to twelve o'clock. Alcazaba and Gibralfaro are both on the line of two o'clock, with Gibralfaro the furthest away. The Cathedral is very nearby at one o'clock, with the Roman Theatre a little way past it and slightly to the right at about one thirty. The Episcopal Palace is due north at twelve o'clock, with the commercial heart of the town on the same bearing, lying between you and the Palace. On your left, at about nine o'clock and some distance along a major street called the Alameda Principal is El Corte Ingles, whilst diametrically opposite at three o'clock and a little way along a tree-lined thoroughfare called Paseo de Espana you'll find the Town Hall with its lovely gardens. Further out in the same direction is the Plaza de Toros, or Bull Ring and behind you at six o'clock is the harbour, where your ship lies peacefully at rest awaiting your return. At four o'clock and on the seafront is the city beach called Playa de la Malagueta, and wherever you've berthed you'll find that this is within easy walking distance of your ship.

So much for the orientation. Let's imagine that you've reached the Dock Gates and that you're in Plaza de la Marina. The first tip is to watch the traffic here, because it crosses this square in every direction and all the cars seem to travel at one hundred miles an hour or more: and, for most of us anyway, it travels on the wrong side of the road! Cross the pedestrian crossing obeying the lights – it really is much safer!
The oldest and most interesting part of the city – the part that is home to the Cathedral, the City Hall, the Alcazaba, Gibralfaro Castle and the Roman Amphitheatre all lie ahead of you or to your right, whilst the newer parts of the city and its commercial heart lie ahead of you and to your left.
Most of the city is within walking distance, so I'll start by walking through some of the sights before touching on those that might require you to take some form of transport.

Two busy roads trend eastward from Plaza de la Marina: that nearest the waterfront is called Paseo de Los Curas, and the landward one which runs parallel is Paseo del Parque. Between them runs the pedestrianised walkway called Paseo de Espana and this is a pleasant place to stroll, shaded as it is by tall palms and massive plane trees. It is a favourite spot for the locals, who gather here to sit and watch the world go by. It is often the site of temporary exhibitions, book fairs and the like. Two thirds of the way along its length on the left hand side, you'll find Malaga's Ayuntamiento, or Town Hall, notable because it is surrounded by rather beautiful, formal gardens lying in the shadow of the Alcazaba, towering just overhead.
Inside the gardens there is an aviary, and parts of the Town Hall are open to the public.

At the eastern end of the Paseo is another busy roundabout, the Plaza del General Torrijos, and the Bullring lies just beyond. If bullfighting is your thing, then you'll might like to know that there is a Museum dedicated to the sport sited within the Plaza de Toros complex – myself, I'd abhor this particular Spanish custom and leave this 'sport' well alone, so consequently can't tell you much about the museum or its exhibits.

Malaga's cathedral is known affectionately as 'La Manquita', the 'Little One Armed Lady'. In reality it is anything but little, but it does only have one belfry and clock tower, hence the name – evidently, the builders ran out of money so that the second, planned, tower never got off the ground. One-armed or not it is a quite magnificent structure, incorporating Renaissance, Baroque and Neo-Classical Styles all rolled into one. It is located just to the northeast of the Plaza de la Marina and within easy walking distance and you can't miss it, because the single tower beckons like a beacon. Head towards it from the Plaza and you're on a street called Molina Lario: at the far end of this (not far at all, by the way) another street called Postigo de Los Abades creates a 'T' junction and here, in the building on your right which stands on the corner, you'll find an excellent Internet Café – just in case you feel the need to surf the net before visiting the Cathedral. La Manquita is worthy of a little of your time for it is a splendid place with three vaulted aisles decorated with cupolas that are studded with palms fronds, shells and other motifs, all supported by classic Corinthian columns. Antique choir stalls which date back to the 1600s sport figures carved by Pedro de Mena, and the pulpit is of delicate rose stone. There is a magnificent pipe organ, and a statue of the Virgin Mary presented to Malaga by Ferdinand and Isabela to commemorate their successful recapture of the city from the Moors. It is possible to take a guided walking tour through the Cathedral, and there is a Cathedral Museum which is home to a number of ecclesiastical treasures.

La Manquita is enormous and in its shadow lie a maze of narrow streets, many of them almost blocked by the pavement cafes that always seem to be teeming with people, locals and tourists alike, sipping coffee, reading the papers, eating tapas or simply watching the world go by. Just outside the massive, main doors is a pretty square called Plaza de Obispo and this, too, is a place where you can pause awhile, slake your thirst, and contemplate the enormity of the church. Close at hand on the northern side of Plaza del Obispo is the 18th century Episcopal Palace, part of which is open to the public.

A short distance beyond La Manquita and to its northeast stands the Palacio de Buenavista, a fine Renaissance building that houses the Picasso Museum. Pablo Picasso was born here and lived locally until the age of fourteen, when he moved away. The Museum has a large collection of the artist's work, most of which was donated by his daughter-in-law. You can also visit his house, a relatively humble shrine which stands on the Plaza de la Merced, two or three blocks further northwards still. Admission to the house is free, but don't go there expecting to see a vast collection of the artist's works, for there are very few in evidence. It literally is the house where he was born and where he lived until moving to Barcelona at the age of fourteen, and I personally found it a little disappointing: the Museum has much more to offer.

I've already mentioned the Roman Amphitheatre, which lies at the foot of the hill on which stand the Alcazaba at the lower level and Gibralfaro at the upper. Alcazaba is easily accessible on foot, whereas I'd advise you to take a bus or taxi if Gibralfaro is your goal, for the road to the top is long, winding and steep. But you'll find the trip up worthwhile, for at the top of the hill and adjacent to the castle stands the Parador Nacional de Gibralfaro commanding stunning views down over the town, its harbour and the coastline. Gibralfaro itself is open to the public and its fabric is in better condition than that of its lower neighbour. Here, too, there are wonderful views, so if you're a photographer be sure to your camera with you. Alcazaba, too, is worth a visit: look out for the Moorish influence that is very much a part of the fabric of the fortress and remember that much of that fabric was torn from the Roman theatre below!

The commercial heart of the town lies to the west of the cathedral and comprises several streets, the most important of which is the pedestrianised Marque de Larios which runs from the Plaza de la Constitucion in the north to the Plaza de la Marina in the south. Here you'll find many shops, large and small, and it's a pleasant and bustling place, again liberally supplied with pavement cafes wafting delicious smells of fresh coffee.

Alameda Principal is that busy multi-lane road trending westwards from Plaza de la Marina. Flower and newspaper stalls are strewn along the length of its central island, and if you walk along it for twenty or so minutes from the Plaza you'll reach 'The Drain', a wide, largely dry, waterway that bisects the city from north to south. At this point the bridge over the drain is called the Puente de Tetuan: cross over and in a short distance on your right you'll find El Corte Ingles. I'll dwell no more on this, lest it be suggested that I am in their employ but you now know for sure where it is!

About halfway between Plaza de la Marina and the Puente de Tetuan bridge and on the right hand side heading west, stands Malaga's central market, the Mercado Central de Atarazanas, set back just one block off Alameda Principal: I have no doubt that market lovers will revel in the displays of just about everything there laid out, seemingly just for your pleasure. I don't know what it is, but Continental Markets always seem to be so much more interesting than our own – the fruit stalls are brighter, the vege-tables bigger and more varied and the smoked hams and sausages hang-ing from the rafters absolutely mouth watering: Malaga's is no exception!

The Commercial Harbour is bounded to the east by a massive breakwater, at the landward end of which is a traditional lighthouse towering over the Malaga Yacht Club and Marina. To the eastern side of this is the Malagueta beach and if all you want to do here is enjoy a day in the sun this is a good place to do it. The beach itself is wide and clean and long and it's lined by all manner of waterfront restaurants and bars, cafes and eating houses. Showers to rid your feet of wet sand are liberally dotted along its length, and here and there beachfront barbeques entice strollers with delicious smells that waft on the balmy breeze. The sea is very blue, always seems to be placid and is very Mediterranean: all of this within easy walk of the ship, wherever you are berthed.

I believe that its true to say that many of the thousands who fly into Malaga every year don't stay in the city, heading rather to the resorts of Torremo-linos, Benalmedena, Fuengirola and Marbella. By so doing, I think they are missing out because Malaga itself is, in my opinion, a really pleasant place, offering a wide diversity of interests which have appeal for every-one. But perhaps you've seen it all before, and actually want to go further afield and it is true to say that the Costa del Sol has a great deal to offer – mountains, plains, valleys and beaches; palaces, resorts, monasteries and cathedrals – and all of them are usually bathed in sunlight and rimmed by the sparkling blue waters of the Mediterranean.

So, let's now leave the city for a while, and explore some of the other de-lights of the region. No doubt, your ship will be offering a variety of tours – to Grenada and the spectacular Alhambra; to Marbella, with its high-rise buildings and enormous marinas; to Nerja, with its caves and Balcony of Europe; or to any one of a dozen other resorts, all comprising the holiday playground that is this part of Spain. I can't deal with them all in one short chapter – but I'll tell you about a few of the ones that I particularly like, be-cause I'm sure your ship will have an excursion going there!

In the chapter on Cadiz you may recall I that I spoke about Columbus – how he doggedly pursued his dreams, how he was often humiliated by his monarchs, and how he eventually won their patronage through his sheer persistence. One of the reasons for his success was the fact that the Catholic monarchs eventually succeeded in bringing the 700 years of war-fare, the 'Reconquista', to and end when they secured, finally, the surren-der of Boabdil. the last Moorish ruler on the Peninsular at Grenada in 1492. This momentous event took place at the Alhambra, and there is every probability that you'll be offered the chance to visit it on one of your shore excursions. If so, and you opt to take it, you're in for a treat for it is not only an historic place it is, for Spain, hugely significant and is beautiful as well. It is a two hour coach drive from Malaga, but the journey takes you through stunning scenery as you head northeastward towards the foothills of the Sierra Nevada, that magnificent mountain range that is so often snow-capped: sailing up the coast of Spain, the range really does provide a breathtaking spectacle as it rises majestically above the sparkling waters of the Mediterranean, and if you take the Grenada tour you'll be heading directly toward it. Grenada itself is a fine place, but the appeal of the town is eclipsed by the tracery and splendour of the Muslim architecture of the Alhambra, the Palace of Sultans.

The Palace was built between 1338 and 1390 on the orders of Ibn al-Ahmar, founder of the Nasrid dynasty. Successively, It has been damaged and restored over the centuries, but studying its many faceted wonders it is not too difficult to imagine what it was like at the height of its importance, well over six hundred years ago.

Whilst the whole complex is stunning, it is the arrays of courtyards bounded by delicate columned arcades, beautiful gardens with their ponds and fountains glittering in the sunlight, banks of flowers cascading in colourful profusion over the thousands of tourists who flock here, that are particularly noteworthy. Look especially for the Lion Court: ancient Islamic poems describe this as being 'The physical manifestation of Paradise on earth' and it was here that Boabdil handed over the keys of the City to Ferdinand and Isabela, thereby adding the final Andalucian jewel to the crown of Castile and Aragon.

Nearby you'll see the Generalife, the smaller summer palace that was at one time the residence of kings in need of comfort and refuge, and the Renaissance palace built by Carlos V in the 16th Century. There are several hotels in Grenada itself, and you'll likely be served lunch in one of them before heading back to Malaga through the beautiful, rolling countryside that is Spain.

If Moorish palaces are not to your liking, you might choose to head south along the coast from Malaga to visit that other tourist honeypot hereabouts – Marbella. The coast road offers enticing views of the sea all along its route, which takes you through places which have almost household names, so popular is the Costa del Sol: Torremolinos, Benalmadena and Fuengirola, all hugely popular holiday destinations, their beaches overflowing with visitors from all over northern Europe.

Along your way, take note of the diversity of the architecture: ancient fortresses and stucco lighthouse towers stand cheek-by-jowl with massive apartment houses and leisure complexes, all of which collectively make up the fabric of this ever popular playground.

One of the shore excursion booklets of my acquaintance describes Marbella as being an exclusive village, and whilst that might be an apt description of the city's old quarter, it does take a lot of imagination to see Marbella in those terms. True, it was once just a little sleepy fishing village but, thanks to the myriads of tourists that throng here each year, today it is a thriving, bustling, sophisticated resort, frequented by the rich and the famous. One of the old town squares is the Plaza de los Naranjos – orange tree square – and this is a delight, with its whitewashed houses exactly matching the Spain of your imagination.

In the mountains more or less midway between Malaga and Marbella is Mijas, one of the most gorgeous mountain villages in the whole of the Costa del Sol. Again, it is pretty certain that you'll be offered a tour here and if you want to get away from the sea and savour some mountain air and scenery, then take this one – you certainly won't be disappointed. The drive to Mijas is scenic and absolutely painless and when you get there you'll find it to be just what you expected: quaint streets, whitewashed houses and shady terraces where you can sit and sip a glass of wine as you contemplate views of the shimmering Mediterranean a few miles to the south. A religious shrine called 'The Sanctuary of the Virgin' commands the best view and occupies the best spot – but then this is Spain, and you'd expect it to: go inside and light a candle if you will, perhaps in gratitude for having been allowed to come to this beautiful place!

The summer heat can be quite fierce, and if your feet start playing you up take a Mijas Taxi, a donkey that will take you, unprotesting, on your journey through the village. On one ship where I was lecturing a lady berated me for promoting this mode of transport – but I truly believe that the little donkeys that fill the Mijas Taxi ranks are happy with their lot – they seem to be well looked after, well fed and are the recipients of a huge amount of love and affection from their many passengers: I certainly would not advocate your taking one if I felt that they were being treated otherwise. Judge for yourselves – they are dear little creatures and seem more than happy.

I'll conclude with a few practical tips for you. The local currency is, of course, the Euro, and I've told you how to find El Cortes. But remember that other shops abound, many of them fashionable boutiques – but you'll find that several of them will be closed from 1.30 to 4.30, so you should plan your shopping around those traditional 'siesta' hours (big shops stay open all day). Good buys are leather goods, jewellery, aromatic soaps and bath splashes, copper plates and ceramic figures. Elegant shoes are, of course, a Spanish speciality, as are hand-crafted guitars and basketware. Taxis will be available on the quayside, and are metered, but remember my tip – always establish the fare to your destination BEFORE setting out! Another favourite mode of transport for tourists in Malaga is the horse and carriage and if these are not paraded for you on the quayside as you leave the gangway they will be waiting for you near Plaza de la Marina at the point where the shuttle bus will drop you off. Again, establish the fare!

If you want to eat ashore, seafood is good here, as is paella. If it's really hot, and you want something refreshing, Gazpacho is a mildly spiced, chilled tomato soup, and don't forget to try the Tapas.

Finally, at the end of a long and rewarding day here in the second of our Andalucian ports, relax on deck in the cool of the evening and watch as the lights come on in the town. The fortresses will be illuminated making them stand out in the gloom of evening and as you gaze at them you'll swear that they are tumbling down their hillside into the single, welcoming, arm of 'La Manquita'.

PALMA
Majorca

Bellver Castle

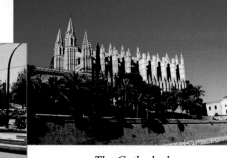

The Cathedral

Paseo des Born

Almudaina Palace

PALMA, Mallorca
Sun, Sand and Sobrasada

Since leaving Malaga, you've sailed deeper into the Mediterranean, plying a north easterly course toward your next destination, Palma de Mallorca, capital of the the Balearic Islands. Although still in Spain, when you reach the island you'll have left Andalucia behind, for Palma is in the autonomous region of Spain called Catalunya.

The island has a land area of just over a thousand square miles, is the largest of the Balearics, and one of the most popular holiday resorts in the whole of the Mediterranean. Every year a myriad tourists flock here – many of them Brits, some, it must be said, lager louts who throng the beaches, night clubs and discos of Magaluf and Palma Nova. But don't, for goodness sake, let the garish images from some of the holiday programmes or the tabloid press deter you, for Palma is a delightful place and Mallorca itself a spectacular island and a beautiful one with an varied topography.

The town with a population of over 300,000 is situated in the south west of the island: it is a cosmopolitan place with stylish shops, a palm shaded seafront promenade, bars and restaurants galore, an attractive Old Quarter and a Gothic cathedral which is beautiful. Millionaires' yachts throng the harbour, and the hustle and bustle of the place is watched over by the imposing serenity of Bellver Castle high on its hillside overlooking the harbour and the city.

I'll take you to Bellver a little later, but its worth this early view from its ramparts for it helps to put the geography of the harbour into perspective.

The promenade forms a grand sweep around the bay: looking at the picture, the cruiseship berths, and there are several for this is a popular cruise destination, are to the right. The one chosen for your ship will depend on two things: the size of the ship, and the availability of berth on the day or your arrival. The largest ships sometimes berth on the western end of the protective harbour mole itself, whilst smaller ones tie up alongside the cruise terminal building. More often than not cruise lines provide a shuttle service into Palma centre, because it is a couple of miles away and a fairly daunting walk, even for the most determined. If you do berth at the terminal itself you'll have an advantage, because it is well equipped with the usual tourist facilities – post office, bureau de change, souvenir stalls and public telephones, whereas the outer berths on the mole are rather more spartan. Taxis will be available on the quayside wherever you are, and they are metered – but do remember to ask the fare in advance if you plan to take one on a journey outside the city limits

Where shuttle buses are provided they'll pick you up on or very near the quayside and you'll be driven along the length of that promenade, passing several major hotels, literally hundreds of yachts of every description many of which can only be described as 'gin palaces', boat repair yards and yacht clubs before you reach the drop off point which is on the waterfront a couple of hundred yards from the cathedral.

Let's start with a stroll around those parts of the city that are within reasonable walking distance, before we venture further afield a little later.
The shuttle stop is on a street called Paseo Sagrera: de-bus here and the cathedral is looming large just in front of you. To reach it, you'll need to cross a couple of busy roads: pedestrian crossings are provided and the local drivers abide by them – but do remember that you are still in Spain and they persist in driving on the wrong side of the road!

'La Seo', a Catalan term that means 'Bishop's See', is the official name of the cathedral and it stands on the site of a former Moorish Mosque in the centre of a pleasant park called Parque del Mar. Construction work on the building was started in the 14th century but it didn't open for business until 1601, and parts of it are still incomplete.
Architecturally, it combines Romanesque with Gothic, and it is visually stunning with soaring pillars and buttresses arching out toward a fountain which is a central feature of the Parque del Mar. The church's interior is divided into a nave and two aisles, with the nave claiming to be one of the highest and widest in the world. A beautiful stained glass rose window dominates the west front and the local bishop presides from a superb marble pulpit. Fifteenth century carvings decorate the choir stalls and there is a serene Baroque cloister. In 1904 one of Spain's most famous sons, the modernist architect Antonio Gaudi, was brought in to oversee several important renovations and the overall effect is magnificent.
In the adjacent Cathedral Museum there is a wealth of ecclesiastical treasures, worthy of a great deal more than a casual glance: among them a solid silver tabernacle used for various processions around the town, several important early paintings, a pair of magnificent candelabra and numbers of religious manuscripts. As I've said, La Seo stands in the pleasant surrounds of the Parque del Mar, the ruffled waters of its fountain reflecting the image of the church. Murals and sculptures in the park are the works of Joan Miro and Josep Guinovart. A stairway leading up from the park takes you to the Almudaina Palace, originally the 11th century fortress residence of the Moorish Caliphs. The structure that you see today was commissioned by James II, who ruled in these parts in the 14th Century. Today, Almudaina is part museum, part headquarters of the Military High Command of the Balearics and part official home to King Juan Carlos when he visits Majorca.

The western side of Parque del Mar is bounded by a fine tree-lined street called Avenida Antonio Maura, which becomes a pedestrian walkway called Paseo des Borne as it trends northwards. In the shade of its mas-

trees you'll find a host of pleasant, open air restaurants, where the 'paella' is, I can assure you, absolutely delicious! On the opposite kerb, immediately alongside the Palace gardens there is a rank where you can pick up a horse and carriage for your tour around the town – check the fares!

Stroll up the street until you reach the point where another road, Calle Conquistadore, forks to the right. Follow this for a hundred yards or so and you'll be in a square called Plaça de Cort, home to a truly ancient olive tree, the site of Palma's City Hall, the Ayuntamiento, and the heart of the Old Quarter. Built in a style known as Palma Baroque which reached the height of its popularity in the 17th century, the building sports an overhanging eave about three metres wide, which is really distinctive. It gives the building a unique and easily recognisable, frontage. Go inside where you'll find a collection of fine paintings by some of Mallorca's most famous sons.

The architecture of the Old Quarter is a wealth of contrasts: from the Baroque of the Town Hall to the Modernist of the El Aguila House with a whole host of styles in between. Walk northwards from Plaça Cort along Calle Colon (Columbus Street): en route look out for the strange and attractive El Aquila House, reminiscent of Barcelona and the works of Antonio Gaudi. In a short distance you'll reach Plaça Mayor, a fine pedestrian square of elegant buildings where clusters of open-air stalls sell all manner of souvenirs, books and bric-a-brac. The local street entertainers are particularly active here, their art honed to perfection – swear that you're looking at a statue, and wonder why it's positioned so awkwardly in the middle of the pedestrian traffic flow – until it moves, to thank a passer-by for the small cash donation deposited in the strategically placed receptacle!

From Plaça Mayor, Las Ramblas, street of flower stalls, strikes northwest and Calle San Miguel heads due north taking you, in short order, to the Market Olivar which will be found on your right. A very short distance beyond and you're in Plaça Espana which fronts Palma's railway station: train buffs will be interested to know that there are two separate railway systems on the island, both of them running into this station – the state run FEVE connects with Inca, a market town in the centre of the island, and the privately owned Soller Railway links Palma with the picturesque north west coast at Soller, about an hour's train ride away.
Retrace your steps to the front of the Almudaina Palace and that tree-lined street of restaurants – you might need a drink by now – and then head northwards once more this time keeping straight ahead instead of turning right into into Calle Conquistador. The street broadens out into an almost park-like area called Paseo des Borne. Bounded by massive trees, and thoughtfully lined with benches where you can perch awhile to watch the world go by, at its north end is a triangular plaza and then Palma's main shopping street, the Avenida del Rei Jaime II: turn left into this and you will

be in the heart of retail-land and most of the better shops. About a half mile along on the left is the Palma branch of that major department store (I hesitate to name it, it's cropped up so often in our chapters so far!)

Leather and suede are good buys here, and gentlemen, if you want to lavish a truly beautiful gift on your lady, cultured Mallorcan pearls are a speciality. Embroidered linen and unusual basketware are worth looking out for and most things can be bought with your favourite plastic. Remember that the local currency is still the Euro (how simple it all is, these days!), and that you'll need some with you for incidentals.

Behind the cathedral and just off the eastern end of the Parque del Mar you'll find the Arab Baths, the last significant remnant of Moorish occupation still in evidence in the city. Look for the distinctive 'horseshoe' shaped arches, a telltale feature of Arab architecture and one that was widely used during the Moors' long stay in Spain.
Still further to the east and at the extremity of Parqe del Mar is the last vestige of the once grand city walls. In 1902 some misguided bureaucrat ordered their demolition and work continued apace until someone saw a little sense and stopped it. The remnant that you see here is all that exists today, a brief reminder of what they must have been like in their heyday.

On the landward side of the waterfront very near the shuttle bus drop off point on Paseo Sagrera you'll find La Lonja, an excellent example of late Spanish Gothic that was built in the early 15th century under the guiding hand of the Mallorcan architect Guillem Sagrera. Square in plan, it has distinctive octagonal towers at each corner and beautiful windows with delicate tracery and ribwork. Sagrera never completed his work for he was called to Naples in 1446 to work on the Castelnovo, leaving La Lonja to be finished by his brother. Today the building is home to periodic art and sculpture exhibitions sponsored by the regional government and if your visit coincides with one of these do take the opportunity to go and see it.Next door stands the Consulado del Mar, originally built to house the local maritime trade authority but which is now used as the seat of the Regional Government.

Art lovers will probably want to visit the Museum of Modern Art, housed in the Sollerich Palace, a mansion in the Old Quarter.

Perhaps you're an enthusiastic lover of churches: if so, then you will already have visited the cathedral and enjoyed its beauty. But there are, of course, many others here. Of particular note is the Church of St. Francis Junipere Serra, the so-called "founder of California" who gave his name to San Francisco. This Gothic building stands a block to the east of Plaça Cort in Plaça San Francisco and is well worth a visit for it has a wonderful,

Baroque altarpiece and beautifully carved choir stalls that date back to the 15th century. Inside is the tomb of a charismatic Mallorcan called Ramon Llul who was something of a mystic, a theologian, avid traveller and respected philosopher who made significant contributions to the Catalan language which was, in his day, somewhat sketchy.

There is much to see here in this city of great variety and vibrant colour all presided over by the cathedral. Most of the sights discussed so far are within walking distance of the bus stop, but there are others that are worth a mention that do require a taxi ride. One of these is that castle that I mentioned right at the beginning which is called, in Catalan, Bellver, meaning 'fine view'. Bellver was built in the early 15th century, and claims to be one of the best preserved fortifications of its type anywhere in the Mediterranean. Originally a Royal Palace, then a prison, and now the home of the Municipal History Museum it is worth a visit, not only for the museum but also for the truly beautiful views from its battlements across the harbour and town. If you want to know what it was like to be imprisoned here, don't miss the dungeons: in one of them, the 18th century reformist Jovellanos was interred when he fell foul of the rulers of his day, and in others can be seen desperate messages scratched into the walls by French prisoners captured by Wellington's troops during the Peninsular Wars.

You may like to take your taxi on to the Spanish Village which is not too far distant. Created in the middle sixties, its concept developed from a similar complex in Barcelona which has proved to be a popular tourist attraction ever since it was built for a World Exposition staged there in 1929. Encircled by a medieval wall, Palma's version consists of a number of churches, houses and palaces representing the architectural styles of all the regions of Spain. Here you can see replicas of the Myrtle Patio in the Alhambra, El Greco's House in Toledo and the Town Hall of Vergara, to mention but a few. The village is really quite comprehensive in its scope, consisting of some fifteen streets, twelve plazas and several 'blocks' of buildings. Browse amongst them, for it is a pleasant and quite relaxing spot to visit. Souvenir stalls sell hand made glass, woodwork, ceramics and leather goods, and there are functioning workshops where you can see craftsmen at work producing some of the goods on display. Obviously, there are restaurants and cafes galore, for the locals will never miss an opportunity to offer you some Tapas!

At the beginning of the chapter, I described the island as having an enormously varied topography, and it does, and a great deal of it is beautiful. Framing the town to the north west are the Tramuntana Mountains and one of the island's most popular tourist destinations nestles in their foothills, Valdemossa, which has attracted visitors for generations. Your cruise will for a certainty have arranged a tour here and if you want to see something of the island as well as a most attractive and quite historic place, then I recommend this one.

The village lies about forty minutes coach drive from Palma, and your route takes you north of the city, through residential areas and industrial estates (and past the local prison) into the countryside where you pass olive and almond groves, orchards and vineyards. Climbing into the hills, you start to see tantalising glimpses of the village between the hills and then, rounding a bend, it's suddenly upon you, perched atop its hillside with the Carthusian Monastery and Church its crowning glory.

Writers, composers, artists and politicians have all lived here, as have royalty, among them the Archduke Luis Salvador of Austria, Edward of England, and the Grand Duke Vladimir of Russia. Revolutionaries like Jovellanos have lived here too, and many of these famous people have stayed in the Monastery which was founded by the Carthusians in 1339. Most of the buildings that you'll see here and walk through today are much later, mainly dating from the 17th century, and were rented out to all these lodgers after the monks departed during a period of anti-clericalism. One of the most famous tenants was Frederic Chopin, who dwelt here for a time during the winter months of 1838-39 with his travelling companion, the writer George Sand. It was here that Chopin penned his rather melancholy 'Funeral March' whilst George, who was deeply disliked by the locals and felt isolated as a result, penned her book 'A Winter in Mallorca' in which she described at some length the hardships of the island.

The locals may have disliked her when she was here, but they have certainly capitalised on the couple's stay ever since, for the two 'cells' that they once occupied in the monastery have been converted into what I suspect are very lucrative museums, and copies of George's book are for sale on every street corner and in every shop. Whilst there are other exhibits in the Monastery, including an art gallery and several rooms devoted to religious art, there is no doubt that the Chopin/Sand combination has become the big attraction and throngs of Chopin's devotees fill their little rooms every day and sometimes visitors are treated to a short concert of his work, ably performed in a theatre created out of one of the larger rooms leading off the main Monastery complex.

Worth seeing, too, is the 18th Century Pharmacy, which proudly displays the philosophy of its founder-monk – "God is the only true medicine" – and the Library, which houses a comprehensive collection of rare books.

The church of the monastery is itself quite imposing, and the surrounding gardens, colourful and lush, fall away down the terraced hillside toward Palma. Valdemossa village is quaint, and offers shopping opportunities for those of you who like to browse: visit it, and you can be sure to leave with memories of mellow rooftops, pretty courtyards and colourful gardens.

Despite being in the mountains, Valdemossa is actually very close to the coast, and the probability is that your tour will take you on the few short miles to the west where the road emerges from the tree-clad hillsides and becomes a clifftop corniche which runs all the way from from Puerto Andratx in the south to Soller in the north, the whole coastline a magnificent vista of cliffs, coves, sea, forests and the occasional mansion of the very rich. One such is La Granja de Esporlas, a 17th century manor which is now a museum dedicated to Mallorcan home life of about two hundred years ago. Here you might stop here for refreshments and have a chance to visit the gardens and grounds and some of the many exhibits which include a typical Mallorcan kitchen of that era, a toy theatre, and a room where local lace makers weave their craft for your enjoyment.

One of the highlights of La Granga is its Cellar and, if given the chance, try some of the delightful Mallorcan wines on offer: they ideally complement the traditional tapas which, doubtless, will also be served.
On the way back to Palma you'll likely stop for a photo-shoot at the Mlrador Ricardo Roca, just south of the little town of Banyalbufar and here you'll marvel at the turquoise ocean lapping at the shoreline about a thousand feet below you.
If your coach follows the southern route home you'll pass through the resort towns of Santa Ponca, Palma Nova and Magaluf – haunt of a myriad holidaymakers, most of them much more noisy than you. You'll be glad that you chose to cruise!

Before we leave Majorca, it would be remiss of me not to mention one of the island's most popular tourist attractions, the extraordinary Caves of the Dragon (Cuevas del Drac) which lie, this time, on the east coast of the island. If caves are your thing, then a visit here is a must. You can take a taxi but again, because they are so popular it is probable that you'll be offered a tour by your ship.

En route to the caves you'll traverse the central 'spine' of the island, the Lianura del Centro, and you'll pass through the villages of Algaida and Villafranca, with their surrounding agricultural lands dotted with windmills The caves were first explored in 1878, but their deeper depths were only opened up twenty-odd years later when researchers finally managed to reach the lowest grottos. The caves stretch for about a mile and a half and are literally littered with stalectites and stalagmites. Trained guides will accompany you and you should be prepared for some quite strenuous walking for there are well over a hundred steps to negotiate. The caves are beautifully illuminated so that you need not fear claustrophobia as, in fact, you don't really feel as if you're underground. Unfortunately, photography underground is not permitted but there are innumerable postcards to be had, so you won't go away from the caves empty-handed. Several rock formations, caverns and pools have been given names like the Sultan's Bath and the Bath of Queen Esther (I like that one!), but the biggest lake which stretches for about six hundred feet is called Lake Martel and given the time you can explore its length by boat. From time to time each day musicians serenade visitors from boats moored on the lake – and the strains of their music wafting through the cavern are quite magical! Well worth the drive and you'll see a lot more of the island at the same time.

You may be travelling as a family, and perhaps by now your children are fed up with cathedrals, palaces and clifftop vistas. Well, naturally, there are lots of attractions here for them but I've chosen just one to tell you about, a waterpark complex called Marineland, which invites its visitors to 'Splash out, and Just Have Fun'. The park is located at Lluc Mayor, close to Palma Nova and a very few miles from Palma and your ship. Like waterparks everywhere, it offers about sixteen different aquatic attractions including waterslides, an adventure river and a surfing beach. As you would expect, there are dozens of restaurants and cafeterias catering to all tastes, so neither you, nor your little ones, will starve!

There is an enormous choice of beaches for you to visit, and the golden sands and glittering sea are the things that made this island so popular in the first place.

Now, harking back to the title of this chapter, we've talked about Chopin and we've talked about Sand – what, you may ask – is Sobrasada? It is a Catalan speciality, particularly favoured on this island: wild boar sausage which is absolutely delicious. If given the chance, taste it, for you'll leave the Balearics with even founder memories.

Time now for us to cruise on!

BARCELONA
Spain

The Sardana

La Sagrada Familia

Arc de Triomf

Santa Eulalia

Las Ramblas

Parc Guelle

Columbus Monument

National Palace

Casa Mila

BARCELONA
Jewel in the Catalan Crown

Barcelona was founded in around 230BC by the Carthaginians, who named it after Hamil Barca, father of Hannibal of elephant fame. In 100 BC the Romans arrived here, establishing their city Augusta Barca which came to play an important role in Rome's eventual overthrow of Carthage. A chequered and often bloody period followed: in the 5th century AD it was invaded by the Visigoths, and then, in the 8th, by the Moors. By this time the local population could be identified as 'Catalans', a people whose origins lay in Southern France – indeed, the Catalan language in common use here has 'Langue d'Oc', the ancient language of Southern France, as its nearest linguistic relative.

The Catalans stemmed the Moorish tide, and nurtured Barcelona as an important port and a major centre with trading links to Ibiza, Sicily, Malta and Menorca. Sadly, its prosperity was not to last. In the early 15th century the city was devastated by the plague and her lucrative trade routes were being progressively undermined by the Genoese, whose determination to build a trading empire in this part of the Mediterranean at the expense of everyone else led to a series of spectacular bank crashes that triggered an almost terminal decline.

In 1492, Boabdil, the last Moorish ruler on the Iberian Peninsular, surrendered the Alhambra at Grenada to the Catholic monarchs Ferdinand and Isabella, bringing to an end the 700 year war of the 'Reconquista'. Unification of a Catholic Spain was complete, and the rulers could turn their attention to matters other than war: amongst other things, they agreed to sponsor a persistent Genoese adventurer, Christopher Columbus, and his epic voyages to the New World led to the transformation of Spain's economy – but Cadiz and Seville were the principal beneficiaries, and Barcelona's decline continued unabated.

Disaffected Catalans took up arms on a number of occasions, but always seemed to back the wrong side – during the War of the Spanish Succession they sided with the Hapsburgs against Felipe V, French contender to the Spanish throne. Suffering siege after siege, the city finally fell in 1714, whereupon Felipe banned the Catalan language, closed Catalan universities, generally made life unpleasant and built a massive fort, the Ciutadella, to keep the rebellious Catalan population in order.

The passage of time gradually saw the lifting of restrictions, and the region's fortunes started to climb out of the doldrums. Trade in local cotton, wine, cork and iron developed alongside a resurgence of the Catalan spirit which blossomed into nationalistic fervour with the Catalan Renaissance of the 1830s, despite French occupation during the Napoleonic Wars.

The population exploded, rising from a mere 115,000 in 1800 to more than half a million in 1900. Spain's Second Republic was formed in 1931 and within days Catalan Nationalists declared a republic within an 'Iberian Federation'. Catalunya then enjoyed a period of genuine autonomy, but the Republican movement right across Spain was dogged by political infighting and Barcelona, its last stronghold, fell to Franco's forces in January 1939 when thousands of Catalans fled to France, Andorra and elsewhere. Franco in his turn banned Catalan, and flooded the region with impoverished Andalucians in the hopes that by so doing he would stamp out, for all time, this troublesome people. But his plan backfired, for the immigrants became more Catalan than the Catalans themselves and when Franco finally popped his clogs he was barely in the grave before Catalunya revived with a vengeance.

The Generalitat, or local parliament, was re-instated, and people gathered all over the region to join in the Sardana, a dance of National Unity. Today, the Catalans still dance it whilst they talk of independence, but it remains just that – talk. Their city is the most important of the region, is the second largest in all of Spain, with a population of 3 million, and can rightfully claim to be one of the most beautiful cities in Europe.
So ends the history lesson.

Such has been its advance that the city was chosen to host the 1992 Olympics, and that inspired a new waterfront, modern access roads, state-of-the art museums and galleries and re-vitalised urban spaces that are, truly, a dream. You'll love it here! Barcelona is a thriving, modern port, and I'm going to spend the next few minutes putting it into some semblance of geographic perspective for you.

The harbour is bounded by a street called the Passeig de Colon: as it progresses east and west it goes by different names, but we are concerned with its pivotal point, the Columbus Monument, standing at the foot Las Ramblas, that ubiquitous highway that forms the principal artery of every large Spanish city. If your cruise line offers a shuttle service into town it is probable that it'll drop you off near the monument, where you'll be strategically placed for your adventures into town on foot and I'll deal with that first. Go inside the Columbus Monument which is open daily and ride an elevator to the top for quite spectacular views across the harbour and over Las Ramblas. Near the monument stands Barcelona's Marina, called Port Vell, home to a multitude of restaurants, an IMAX cinema complex and the largest aquarium in Europe. A model submarine outside the cinema is popular with younger visitors, whilst those who love things nautical will gravitate to the nearby Royal Drassanes Maritime Museum, an important feature of which is the medieval shipyard where the galleys that helped to make Barcelona a great seaport in the first place were built. Founded in the mid-13th century, the Drassanes dockyard is the largest and most complete existing example of its type anywhere in the world, and is worth visiting. Among the vessels built here was "Real", flagship of Don Juan of Austria who led the Christian fleet to victory at the Battle of Lepanto of 1571. In the museum, authentic pre-Colombian maps are displayed along-side all manner of maritime artefacts that really are a magnet for lovers of ships and the sea from very far and wide.

Not far from the Marina is La Ciutadella, site of that castle that I mentioned – the one built by Filipe V as a means of controlling a restless population. The citadel itself has long gone, but the park that remains is quite beauti-ful, and was in fact created for a Universal Exposition that was staged here in 1888. It is also home to the Parliament of Catalunya, and, at the extreme northern end, Barcelona's answer to the Arc de Triomph, in this case the 'Arc de Triomf'!

Now walk northwards up Las Ramblas and in a short distance you'll have on your right the Gothic Quarter, the oldest part of the city. The buildings here date mainly from the 13th century and the whole area exudes a truly medieval atmosphere. Centrally stands the Cathedral of Santa Eulalia (not to be confused with La Sagrada Familia – more about that later).

Built between 1298 and 1454 on the site of an ancient Roman temple dedi-cated to Hercules, Santa Eulalia was named after the 13 year old martyr whose sarcophagus, carved in bas-relief with scenes of her torture and execution, can be seen inside. Outside, the Cathedral is in the classic, Catalonian Gothic style, whilst inside a single, wide nave and twenty eight side chapels are set between slender columns supporting a vaulted ceiling that soars eighty five feet overhead. There is a magnificent 500 year old stained glass window and a Sacristy Museum whose centrepiece is an 11th century baptismal font. Lovers of churches and things ecclesiastical will revel in a visit here.

Placa del Rei, the Square of the Kings, is a gracious square whose Gothic buildings include the Palau Major, former residence of Catalan royalty.

City Hall stands in the nearby Placa Sant Jaume and if you walk eastwards about three blocks along Marques Dellio you'll reach the Picasso Museum one of Barcelona's most popular attractions. Housed in five adjoining me-dieval palaces at Carrer Montcada, the museum opened its doors in 1963 with works donated by Jaime Sabartes, a long time friend of Picasso. When Sabartes died in 1968, Picasso himself donated paintings and other early examples of his work and these were augmented by works left by the artist himself in his will. There are two main sections: paintings and drawings, and ceramics. The most famous work on view is a series of 44 paintings called Las Meninas.

Nearby is the Palau de la Musica Catalana, or the Palace of Catalan Music which stands near a little square called the Plaça Lluis Millet. The guidebooks describe this as a 'real palace of music, a Modernist celebration of tilework, sculpture and stained glass'. Completed in 1908, its elaborate red-brick façade is lined with mosaic covered pillars and topped by the busts of the great composers. Inside, the auditorium is lit by a huge inverted dome of stained glass depicting angelic choristers. Completed in 1908, its elaborate red-brick façade is lined with mosaic covered pillars and topped by the busts of the great composers. Inside, the auditorium is lit by a huge inverted dome of stained glass depicting angelic choristers.

Las Ramblas is worthy of a few words, for it is a fine, tree-lined, bustling, pedestrianised street, the busiest in all of the city, full of flower stalls, colourful markets and myriads of people. Half way along its length, this time on the left, you'll find the best of Barcelona's markets, the Boqueira, which sells just about everything in the way of fruit, vegetables, knick-knacks and wine. In the street itself curiosity shops, up-market boutiques, restaurants and souvenir stalls stand cheek by jowl, and the parading masses can watch pavement artists, gaze at tattooists, wonder at street performers and even listen to visiting didgerydoo players performing their art with an abandon seldom found so far away from Ayers Rock. All human life seems to be here – as is, it must be said, the odd opportunist pickpocket: be warned!

At the head of Las Ramblas stands Plaça Catalunya, named after this region of Spain, this square is home to gardens, fountains, statues, people and pigeons – thousands of them, just like Trafalgar Square back home. The shoppers amongst you will want to know that the square is also home to El Corte Ingles which occupies most of the eastern side of the plaza! It might be useful to know that the street adjacent to the shop is the principal terminal for the open-topped Tourist Buses that'll take you on comprehensive tours of the city: there are two routes, essentially one heading east and north, the other heading west and south. Both of them offer an excellent opportunity to see the sites without wearing out shoe leather, and they are relatively inexpensive.

Now Barcelona is a big city and by the time you reach Catalunya you will have already walked some distance. But, no doubt you're aching to know whether you're within striking distance of that most famous of the city's landmarks, Gaudi's fantastical La Sagrada Familia. Well, you are – just. It stands about twelve city blocks further northwards: if you plan on walking it, I hope you've got comfortable shoes. One way or the other, you must see it – no one comes to Barcelona without paying the place a visit. Walk it, and be prepared for sore feet. Or, take a cab or one of the Tourist Buses just described. Or, better still, take one of the tours that undoubtedly the ship will be offering you – that way, you'll have the services of a guide, and La Sagrada is most certainly worthy of one! Because of those twelve city blocks, I deem it to be just beyond normal walking range, so I'll deal with it just a little later. But just in case you are determined to walk, then about half way there you'll come across that other landmark common to most Spanish cities, the Plaza do Toros, or Bullring, which stands one block to the south of Barcelona's longest street, the Avenida Diagonal which trends right across the city from north west to south east.

Some distance to the north and west of Plaça Espana, lovers of football will find Nou Camp, home to FC Barcelona and one of the largest football stadiums in Europe – more about this in a little while.

The western side of the city is dominated by Montjuic, which is home to many of the principal attarctions: the National Palace with its grandiose fountains houses the Museum of Catalunyan Art whose collection of Romanesque items, centered around a series of wondrous 12th century frescoes, is said to be the finest anywhere in the world. There is also a significant Gothic collection, and a Renaissance section displaying works by El Greco, Velazquez and Zurbaran.

Nearby is the Pueblo Espanol, or Spanish Village, another exhibit which was created for the 1929 Exposition but one which has endured as an attraction down into our day. In here you can study the architectural styles and cultures from all the regions of Spain, comparing, for example the architecture of Catalunya with that of Galicia, and you can enjoy a browse through the souvenir shops for that all important memento of your visit.

Slake your thirst with a cup of coffee or glass of wine in one of the many open-air cafes and restaurants that abound before heading for the Foundation where the works of Joan Miro, (1893 – 1983) one of the most famous of all Catalunyan artists, is housed. Miro always remained a Catalan painter, but he developed a surrealistic style characterised by bright, vibrant colours and amazing forms which may not be entirely to your taste but are nonetheless worth seeing.

The Archaeological Museum displays artefacts from pre-history through the Visigothic period, whilst the Ethnological Museum boasts items from Oceania, Africa, Asia and Latin America.

So far, quite deliberately, I've refrained from mentioning one of Barcelona's most famous sons, Antonio Gaudi, and I have done so because a casual glance at his many and quite extraordinary works certainly does him no justice – they are worth a full scale, dedicated tour, and if your cruise line is not offering such an excursion, I'll eat my hat.

Gaudi's crowning glory is that very symbol of Barcelona, Europe's most unconventional church, the Temple Expiatori de La Sagrada Familia or the Holy Family Church, to give it its full name.
Undoubtedly one of Antonio Gaudi's most famous works, construction of a church was started on this site in 1882 but work stumbled and when Gaudi was approached he agreed to take over as architect in 1883 on the condition that he was given a free hand in the building's design. His wish was granted, and the extent of his freedom is in evidence at every turn. For him, La Sagrada became an obsession. He lived on site here, as a recluse, for some 16 years and was buried in the crypt following his death in a road accident in 1926.

Still unfinished, work continues on this truly fascinating place, its profuse decoration surreal in the extreme. The Nativity façade was completed in 1904, and features scenes from Christ's nativity and childhood, whereas the so-called Passion façade was completed in the late 1980s: close examination reveals the huge differences in style between these two facades which nonetheless blend into a convincing whole. The astonishing structure is a very long way from being complete: in fact, completion will be impossible until the leases on all the buildings on the south side of the site expire, allowing their demolition – and this will not happen for several more years as yet. In the meantime, work goes on and is funded by public subscription and by the admission charges levied upon all those who venture inside the perimeter fences. Visit it you must – but my advice is to be content with the outside, because sightseers inside are greeted with an enormous building site. If you do want a different perspective of that site, you can take elevators up into those towers that are complete, by doing so providing yourself with a bird's eye view – of the same building site. Eight of the towers have been completed out of the twelve that are planned (one for each of the apostles), so it is evident that there is a long way to go – and it is estimated by some that it could take another fifty years before the church officially opens its doors to worshippers.

Trending northwards from our old friend the Plaça Catalunya is a major street called Passeig de Gracia, and it is on this that several of Gaudi's other famous buildings may be found. On the left heading towards the Avenida Diagonal is the extraordinary Casa Battlo, then further along, on the right, La Pedrera, the so-called Stone Quarry, an apartment house which Gaudi created in the first decade of the 20th century. Faced with buildings like these, one could be forgiven for wondering what it was that inspired this man. He was born in Tarragona and served his time as a blacksmith's apprentice before going on to study at Barcelona's School of Architecture. It is said that that he was driven by a fierce, individualistic, nationalism which transcended a romantic view of a medieval past and that it was this that nurtured in him a style that was entirely his own: no more than a casual glance at La Sagrada or Casa Mila confirms that he was absolutely unique. At the time of its construction, Casa Mila represented a major departure from the accepted architectural practices of its day, and when first unveiled Gaudi was ridiculed. But today, the building is recognised as being a supremely innovative structure, its façade an impressive, wave-like, mass of rough-chipped stone. You can visit the roof and gaze at chimneys which have such an intimidating and grotesque appearance that they are called 'witch scarers'! In 1984, the building was designated a World Heritage site by UNESCO.

No self-respecting Gaudi Tour would miss Parc Guell, an area lying well to the north of the city which started life as a carefully planned enclave for the very wealthy. The plan was ill conceived and its residential objectives were never achieved, but it did become a living testament to the works of Gaudi, and is arguably his most colourful creation. Another World Heritage site, a browse through its peaceful environs leads you to ever more extraordinary pavilions, stairways, winding paths and squares. Look for the Pinnacle and the Gran Placa Circular, a snaking, massively decorated bench which measures one hundred and fifty two metres in length and is said to be the longest in the world. Seek out the Room of a Hundred Columns, a covered market hall of 84 crooked pillars decorated with glass and ceramic mosaics. Wander through Parc Guell for yourself – I can guarantee that every corner you go around will bring you more delight!
Those works mentioned here are by no means the only ones – whole books are devoted to 'The Barcelona of Gaudi', but it unlikely that you'll have the chance to see any more than some of those described!

Artworks, architecture, cathedrals and museums have dominated our discussion so far, and cruise lines do know that many of their passengers will either have seen them all before and are in search of something entirely different. For this reason they do like to offer variety in their excursions, and in all probability you'll be given a chance to do something altogether different during your stay here.

Football lovers will probably be offered a chance to visit Nou Camp, home to 'Barca', or FC Barcelona. The club has around a hundred thousand members, and its stadium on the western side of the city was built in 1957. Success and growth prompted expansion so that it had to be extended in 1982, and today it can accommodate ninety eight thousand fans, seated! Typically, tours here will take you through the changing rooms and out onto the hallowed ground itself by way of the players' corridor. In the Press Room your photograph will be taken, just as though you were a member of one of the competing teams, and you'll be conducted through the VIP stalls before being taken to the Barca Museum with its arrays of memorabilia. In the souvenir shop you'll have ample opportunity to buy something to remind you of your visit, and you'll no doubt return to your ship wishing that your local club had something similar.

You may want to look a little further afield. High above the city and to its north west is an area called Tibidado where the visitor can ride a funicular railway to a popular amusement park which offers many attractions, amongst them an excellent science museum which provides all sorts of interactive, hands-on experiences and a fine planetarium offering varied shows. The area is crowned by the Church of the Sacred Heart which is topped by a huge figure of Christ: for really spectacular views of the city, ride the elevator up to his feet.

Finally, you may just want to chill-out in the Costa Brava sun. If you do, there will probably be a 'Day by the Beach' tour which may even include a boat ride along the sun drenched coastline of the Costa Brava. Barcelona's main beach is called Platja Gran, and it lies at the centre of the resort of Tossa de Mar where, apart from the sea and the sand, you'll be able to explore the old part of the town with its winding cobbled streets and ancient houses. But, it's the beach that is the attraction on this tour: lie in the sun (take lots of sun cream!), enjoy the lunch that will probably be included in the price, and think of all your fellow passengers rushing about in the city in their pursuit of culture!

In much the same vein you could visit the waterpark which is a feature of Isla Fantasia. A tour to this will take you away from your ship for something like seven hours, but you can be assured that they will not be boring! You'll be left to your own devices at Fantasy Island, which offers no less than twenty one different attractions, including Torpedo Slides, Grand Rapids, Double Spirals, Aquamania, Kamikazes and a Super Slide, all of which sound hectic, exciting and fun: but, being of the age that I am, you might rightly conclude that I've never been!.

Barcelona is a superb, vibrant and beautiful city. Your visit by ship will of necessity be brief, and it will not allow you to do much more than scratch the surface, much as I have done in this chapter. But, if I've been able to fill you with anticipation for an excellent port on your cruise itinerary, then I will have achieved my objective.

Hola!

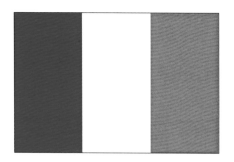

LIVORNO
(for FLORENCE & PISA)
Italy

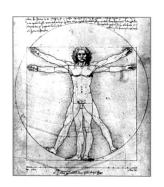

David - Michelangelo

Florence Panorama

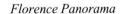

Pitti Palace

Ponte Vecchio

Santa Maria dei Fiore

Santa Croce

Baptistry, Pisa

The Boar

Pisa – the Cathedral & Campanile

LIVORNO
Gateway to Florence – birthplace of the Renaissance

Having spent the better part of this book so far in Spain, we're now going to leave it and head eastwards across the Mediterranean for Livorno, which lies on the west coast of Italy. Arriving there, you'll find yourselves in a very special part of the country with your immediate destination, Livorno, one time known to the British as Leghorn, its principal port. Look at any map, and you'll see it's not hard to find Livorno and Florence, Pisa, San Gimignano and Volterra, important places all, here in Tuscany. This is a beautiful land – a land of mountains and rugged coastlines, the Chianti Hills, and Carrara marble – and its beauty is the result of eons of careful husbandry of olives, vines and other crops, all of them bathed in a natural light that seems uniquely Tuscan. This is the land which gave birth to the Renaissance – the rebirth – that era which paved the way for the modern world when Europe climbed out of the darkness of the middle ages into the age of enlightenment. In his paintings Giotto projected Tuscany into space, whilst Brunelleschi crowned space with his magnificent feat of Renaissance engineering, the spectacular Dome of Florence's cathedral

What of these cities – places that speak of great architecture, many of them one time homes of noble families like the Urbinos and the Medici, and many of them the guardians of some of the greatest artistic and literary masterpieces ever created – from Michelangelo's 'David' to Dante's 'Divine Comedy', and a huge host of others in between: we'll talk of some of them in depth.

What of the people? They are proud, wary of strangers and chic – if you don't believe me, go and see Florence, which is nothing if not chic – and they are passionate: stand in awe before Botticelli's Madonna if you want proof of that. They are a people possessed of a sense of place, of family, and of craftsmanship, all things that help to create the Tuscan miracle. I've said that they are wary of strangers but they are invariably polite, wanting to make a good impression and they are a good looking people: traditional Etruscan looks – "full dark eyes, pointed beards, long inquisitive noses and the Mona Lisa smile" (how H V Morton sums them up) – can still be found here, and you're going to visit the town and the people – what a treat in store!

Livorno is our gateway to all this, and we are following in a long tradition of tourists visiting Tuscany – from some of the of the great literary figures of our time, people like Byron, Shelley, D H Lawrence and Virginia Woolfe – to the thousands of British tourists who come each year for the colour, the festivals and that certain Tuscan style – many of them Brits, some of whom buy permanent homes in the region, settle down and try to capture the

Tuscan dream. A friend called Bob Snelling coined a term for the land that these incomers have helped to create – 'Chiantishire' – an archipelago of foreigners in the Chianti hills: Germans, Swiss, French as well as the English – art lovers, academics on sabbaticals and gourmets adding anti-pasta to their repertoires – not forgetting, of course, those intent upon Relocation! Relocation! Relocation! Some of these folk have taken to living in the cities, but most of them end up on isolated farms where, in the interests of 'going native' they tolerate faulty electricity, brackish well water and shifty tradesmen: they learn Italian, enrol their children on art courses, form clubs and societies and hope to meet celebrities. For the most part they despise tourists and pretend to be Italian and more especially, Tuscan. When you get here you'll understand why, because it is lovely, as you'll see as you explore a very exciting part of Italy, not as tourists who have come to gawp, but as travellers who want to observe, analyse and understand. Here, in Michelangelo's terms, you'll find no agony – only ecstasy!

It was in 1406 that Florence successfully defeated its rival city, Pisa: the Florentines wanted its harbour. Unfortunately for them, the harbour silted up rendering it useless, so in 1421 they bought Livorno, which in those days was little more than a swamp, from Genoa. Today, it is Italy's third largest port with a population of approximately 200,000 and the province in which it lies is noted for its wine, sandy beaches, links with Napoleon and its fish soup, cacciucco, consisting of different kinds of fish mixed in with, tomatoes, chillies, parsley and toasted bread – delicious! In all, not a bad buy for the 100,000 florins that the Florentines paid!

In 1571, Cosimo I created a modern port and city, star shaped with five bastions, and by the 19th century it boasted cosmopolitan salons, elegant avenues and some fine villas, and it became a very important part of the Grand Tour. Today much of that grandeur has gone, helped on its way by almost a hundred allied bombing raids in World War II and the determined efforts of the German Army. So, you'll be arriving at a modern city, which thrives on commerce rather than tourism, and one that has but few traces of its former, grander, days. It is true that most people pass through Livorno to more interesting places, but there are things to see here, so for a few minutes I'll dwell on them for the benefit of those who don't want to travel further afield, or who have done so before.

The port is a ten to twenty minute walk from the town (depending on where you berth), and to get there you stroll across a bridge alongside the fishing harbour and then up to the Via Grande which leads you directly to the town centre. If you're on a larger ship you might have to berth further out and your ship will probably provide the usual complimentary shuttle service into town. You'll find that is a ten minute bus ride, during which you'll have glimpses of the Old Fort, Fortezza Vecchia with its Medici Walls, and the

Fortezza Nuova or New Fort, which was built in 1590 and is today a modern conference centre. The Via Grande is the principal shopping street, and the cathedral stands in the nearby Piazza Grande, whilst the Town Hall is, logically, in the Piazza Municipo. Between the Old and New Forts you'll find an attractive district called Venezia with a market, massive Piazza della Republica, an Aquarium and a Promenade.

Your shuttle bus will drop you near the Town Hall, and you'll be pleased to know that there is a useful Tourist Information kiosk immediately to hand. Sometimes, the port authority provides essential information and port maps on the quayside, and a map is useful if you're going to explore locally – your ship may even provide you one, saving you the hassle.

The Town Centre is only a matter of yards from the shuttle bus stop, and at its heart is the Cathedral, dedicated to St Francis of Assisi. The brainchild of an architect called Alesandro Pieroni, work on the building was started in 1581 and completed in 1606. The building was heavily damaged in World War II and although it's quite modest and unpretentious it is worth a look. There are two good shopping streets near the Square – the Via Grande and the Via Cairoli.

To the left of the Cathedral is a an open air market and, if it's market day, you'll find a feast of colour, noise and excitement: if it's not market day, you will have to be content with the nearby covered market, which is a little less appealing, but pleasant enough. It occupies a 19th century building the outside of which is decorated with carvings of sheaves of corn and fish, the inside awash with all manner of vegetables, hams, cheeses and fish, all displayed with some of that Italian flair I spoke about at the beginning.

A short walk from the market will bring you to Piazza Cavour, where you'll find the main Tourist Information Office and then in the massive Piazza della Republica, whose name is rather more exciting than its reality, you'll see statues of Kings Ferdinand III and Leopold II, both of them dressed as Roman consuls. From here can be seen the walls of the New Fort situated on a canal, to the left of which is a bridge: cross over, and discover the Venezia area, so called because with a lot of imagination it looks a little like Venice: it abounds with boats, bridges, workshops and a fascinating labyrinth of streets, and it is in here that that map that you picked up will come in handy!

This area is famous hereabouts for the Carnevale Marinaro, a water pageant of boats and swimmers held every year on the first Sunday in July. Try to navigate your way back to the Old Port, and walk the length of those Medici Walls to the fishermens' stalls that line the quayside.
If you then cross the road you will be back at the bottom of the Via Grande

with its fine arcades and shops and from there you'll easily find your way back to Piazza Grande and your shuttle bus stop.

There is a newly restored Museum in Livorno, and the Promenade is quite impressive – but it is at least a 20 minute walk from the Old Fort or Via Grande so if you want to see it, I'd advise a taking a taxi. Nearby you'll find sun-bathing facilities and a swimming pool, but if you want to swim in the sea you'll have to seek some directions from the Tourist Office, for the nearest beaches are some distance away.

Near the Promenade stands the Church of San Jacobi and the Naval College, and I've already told you where the best shops are: normal shopping hours are 9am to1pm and 4pm to 8pm, and good buys are fashions, textiles, leather, pottery and ceramics as well as wine, oil and honey: all of these of good quality.

If you decide to stay here you can have an interesting day, but I feel sure that you'll want to go further afield – perhaps to Pisa, or more likely, Florence, for there is no doubt that the real wonders of Renaissance Italy lie beyond Livorno's city limits.

No cruise line worth its salt would come to Livorno without offering at least one excursion to Florence, and most of them run several, so you're likely to be spoiled for choice. But do be advised that you can get there, and to Pisa, independently. Take a No. 1 bus from Piazza Grande in Livorno to the train station, from which trains run frequently to Pisa, a mere twelve miles away. Once you get there, you'll face a good twenty five minute walk to the Field of Miracles (about which much more, later), but apart from this, the journey is painless. Similarly, you can get to Florence by train, but this time the journey is more like seventy miles. Either way, do plan your journeys carefully and remember, there is nothing quite so disconcerting for a cruise passenger as arriving back at the quayside to see you ship gently disappearing over the horizon – and be warned, it won't wait for you if you're late! On the other hand, if you're on a ship's tour which is delayed by traffic or whatever, the ship will always wait: incentive indeed!

The early history of Florence is in some dispute: there is evidence of a settlement on the banks of the Arno river dating back to about 1000 BC, and the earliest inhabitants could have been native Italics or Etruscans. Whoever they were, there is no doubt that the Etruscans came to prominence here and Faesulae, Florence's present day suburb of Fiesole, was an important city in its own right and the northernmost member of the Etruscan Dodecapolis. In 59 BC, Julius Caesar set up a colony in these parts for army veterans, and he called it Florentia, which in time was corrupted to Fiorenza, and finally became the Fiernze (Florence) of today.

By the 1100s, Florence was the leading city of the County of Tuscany, and a momentum of growth was in train: in the 1170s, new city walls were needed to enclose a place which, by then, was rapidly becoming one of the biggest cities of Europe. Much of the growth could be attributed to the textile industry – the weaving and finishing of cloth from wool, not only from Tuscany but shipped, too, from as far away as Spain and England. The gain from this trade was managed by the guilds, and led ultimately to even more profitable businesses – banking and finance. Faction fighting between noble families was rife through the 12th and 13th centuries but despite this the city's wealth and population grew enormously throughout the 1200s. Trade contracts spread Europewide, and crowned heads from just about everywhere took out loans from Florentine banks, which were ever ready to oblige. In 1235, the city minted modern Europe's first gold coin, the *florin,* which became a standard unit of currency right across the continent. Burgeoning opulence led to new opportunities for culture and art, with the city's golden age starting in the 1290s – the decade which saw an enormous public building programme, including the Pallazo della Signoria, the Cathedral and great churches such as Santa Croce.

The Black Death struck in 1348, proving to be a blow from which the city struggled to recover. Faction fighting and wars compounded a decline until 1434, when Cosimo de' Medici, who happened to be the head of Florence's largest bank, was called to power. He instituted some real reforms, including the introduction of a progressive income tax that reduced the tax burden on the poor and effectively muted class conflict. The faction fighting declined, and when Cosimo died in 1464 his tomb was inscribed 'Pater Patriae' (Father of the Nation) and there was practically no dissent when his son Piero took over the reigns of power. Piero died of gout in 1469, and was succeeded by his son Lorenzo who remained in power for twenty three years, becoming known almost universally, as 'The Magnificent'. He was at the helm for the height of the Florentine Renaissance, during which the city became the artistic and cultural centre of Europe. Donatello, Michelangelo and Leonardo da Vinci all worked here, as did so many others, and their art has dominated Florence ever since.

Gian Gastone, the last Medici, died in 1737, by which time the fate of Tuscany had been decided by the great powers of Europe and rulership passed to Francis Stephen, Duke of Lorraine. Napoleon ruled for a time and then, in 1861, Florence finally became part of the united Italy. So you can see that it has had a long and chequered history.

Massive floods in 1966 caused tremendous damage to buildings and works of art, and the international community rallied to assist in the restoration. Today the city is magnificent, with a population of 500,000. UNESCO estimates that Italy possesses 60% of the world's most import-tant works of art, and half of these are in Florence and the Uffizi Gallery, which surpasses a mass of other local museums, all superb in their own right, can hold its head high alongside the likes of the Metropolitan in New York and the Hermitage in St Petersburg, and ranks as one of the greatest museums in the world.

The River Arno divides the city in two with the northern district dominated by the Duomo and the Piazza Della Signoria, whilst the Oetrano district to the south boasts Santo Spirito and the Pitti Palace, one time home of the Medici family. Several bridges connect the two sides, the most famous being the Ponte Vecchio, built by Taddeo Gaddi in 1360. Today, the bridge is still home to the jewellers and goldsmiths whose forebears have occupied its many rooms and shops since the far off days of Cosimo.

As I said a little earlier, you may choose to get to Florence independently by train, or even by taxi, but I'm going to assume that you've decided to play it safe and take the ship's 'transfer' tour – usually called 'Florence on Your Own', or something similar – and in this event you'll get exactly what it says on the tin – a coach transfer to Florence, with the rest of your time there 'on your own'. This is a good option, because it gets you to the city with a minimum of fuss. No doubt, your ship will also offer a number of other combinations of options as well – one that guides you through the major sites and lasts all day is one, another that guides you through some of the sights for part of the day and then leaves you to your own devices for the rest of it is another, whilst yet another might take you to Florence and guide you through the main sights and then take you on to Pisa and do the same there. Whatever you're offered, you'll be away from Livorno and your temporary home for the better part of eight hours. (If you have decided to do it on your own, you're going to arrive at the Florence Railway Station instead of at the coach drop off point, but from then on your way ahead is very similar). I'm not going to talk about these options individually in this chapter; rather, I'm going to assume that you've reached the coach park and are ready for a walking tour through the major sights: when you've done, I'll take you back to the coach for your return journey through the Tuscan countryside.

In my experience, cruise passengers visiting the city are always deposited on a street called Lungarno Pecori Giraldi, where there is provision for a coach to stop temporarily. On the banks of the Arno, the stop is a short distance (about a ten minute walk) to the Piazza Santa Croce, the massive square which stands in front of the magnificent church of the same name. Santa Croce has been described as the Westminster Abbey of Florence. It is the largest Franciscan basilica in Italy, and is a must for everybody visiting here. Work started on the building in 1294, under the direction

70

Arnolfo di Cambio and it was pretty well completed by the 1450s although the black and white, neo-gothic façade was only built in the late 19th century. Inside the church you'll find it to be rather austere, barn-like in some respects, but the 14th century stained glass window is a redeeming feature. Ghiberti, Machiavelli, Rossini, Galileo and Michelangelo are all buried here and as you enter the main doors you'll find the tomb of the latter immediately on your right hand. Michelangelo actually died in Rome, but before his death he consented to being buried in Florence and his tomb was created by Vasari. Still on your right and part way toward the Sanctuary you'll find Donatello's 'Annunciation', and then the marble pulpit which is a masterpiece. Visit the Sacristy with its frescoes by Gaddi, Aretino and Gerini and head for the 'Museo dell'Opera di Santa Croce' which lies between the first and second cloisters: this is home to other fine works of art which should not be missed.

Piazza Santa Croce is bounded by some interesting buildings, including a row of ancient houses with overhanging upper storeys. A rather forbidding statue of Dante stands to the left of the church doors and its base is a popular perch for the throngs waiting to go into the church or simply sitting and enjoying the Florentine sun.

The Horne Museum, named after the English art historian who penned a biography of Botticelli and bequeathed his art collection to the city, lies a short distance towards the river down a street called Borgo Santa Croce. The museum is worth a visit if for no other reason than to see Giotto's beautiful painting of St. Stephen.

Walk westward along Borgo Dei Greci, and in another ten minutes or so you'll reach Piazza della Signora, the civic heart of the city. Here, in 1498, Savonarola, the Dominican Friar who preached radical reform after Lorenzo Medici's passing, was burned at the stake – it certainly has seen less gracious times! It is huge and is dominated by the fortress-like palace and tower which is Palazzo Vecchio, one time seat of government.
Immediately in front of the Palazzo stands a copy of Michelangelo's 'David' – the original was removed to the Galleria dell' Accademia in 1873 for safer keeping, and a mammoth Neptune Fountain created by Ammannati stands on the corner. The Palazzo is the modern day City Hall, and several of its more historical rooms are open to the public.
On the southern boundary of the Piazza stands the Loggia dei Lanzi, easily identified by its three graceful arches. Used originally as a forum for public political speeches, it is today home to an array of sculptures, among them the famous 'Rape of the Sabines', and 'Hercules and Nessus', both by Giambologna.

The pedestrian way that leads south, its entrance between the Loggia and the Palazzo, is Piazzale D' Uffizi: walk down it and on your left stands the collonaded frontage of one of Florence's most famous galleries, the Uffizi, home to almost two thousand works of art that really need weeks rather than hours to do them justice. The Uffizi strives to arrange its works in chronological order with rooms devoted to the 13th and 14th centuries, the early Renaissance and later Renaissance periods: others focus on the works of Botticelli and Mannerism, and yet others are devoted to the paintings of Raphael and the Flemish masters. Naming even the most important art on view is far beyond the scope of this book, but all the reputable guides to Florence will name them for you. If your arrival here is in the height of summer and you are doing the city independently, be prepared for lengthy queues waiting to get into the gallery. (Guided ship's tours usually manage to overcome this irritation).

The south face of the Uffizi fronts onto the River Arno and you access the riverside road, Lungarno Acciaioli, by way of a pedestrian walkway. Turn right, and Ponte Vecchio, in all its ancient splendour, is right ahead. The bridge that you see dates from 1345, although there was an older, wooden one before that which was said to date from Roman times. A 'secret' passage runs over the bridge: originally built for Cosimo, this provided him with direct access from Palazzo Vecchio, through the Uffizi, across the river to the Pitti Palace. Walk over the bridge, home to many a Florentine goldsmith and on the other side you'll be in Via de Guicciardini, which will lead you directly to Piazza Pitti and its Palace. Thought to have been designed by Brunellschi for Luca Pitti, work on the Pitti was started in the mid 1400s but was not finally completed until 1783. The original building was much smaller than the one you see today and it was the Medici family that extended it after they acquired it from the first owners when the latter fell on hard times. The Medicis were also responsible for the beautiful Boboli Gardens that lie behind the palace and are worth a visit. Today the Pitti houses several separate museums – clothes, ceramics, carriages, silver – but it is the Galleria Palatina that is the main attraction, its outstanding collection of 16th/18th century paintings belonging to the Grand Dukes – works by Giorgione, Titian, Rubens, Raphael, Caravaggio, Lippi – just about everyone, in fact – almost beyond belief.

Retrace your steps, back over the bridge, this time keeping straight ahead onto a street called Via Por Santa Maria which will bring you first to the Mercato Nuovo where you'll find the famous bronze boar fashioned by Pietro Tacca: stroke the boar's nose, so they say, and you'll be certain to return to Florence. Then Piazza della Republica, the Via Roma, and Piazza di San Giovanni where stands the Baptistry, and next to it, the Piazza del Duomo, home to the Cathedral of Santa Maria del Fiore. Work on this started in 1296 and it wasn't consecrated until 1436, so it took a little time to build and one of the reasons was that.at the time of its commissioning, it was decreed that "It will be so magnificent that it will surpass anything built by the Greeks and Romans" – and it is superb, despite the fact that one critic described it as looking a little like 'Victorian Wallpaper' with its slightly eccentric façade of green, white and red marble rectangles. It is astonishing: topped as it is by the fabulous dome of Brunelleschi, it is the third greatest church in the world, capable, it is said, of accommodating ten thousand worshippers. Its Gothic interior is magnificent, if a little austere: here you'll find a mural of an English mercenary Sir John Hawkwood and paintings commemorating events in the life of Dante. Stained glass windows are by Ucello, Donatello, Ghiberti and Castagno. But the best of its exhibits have long since been moved to the nearby Museo dell'Opera dei Duomo, including Michelangelo's 'Pieta' and Donatello's 'Mary Magadelene' – try not to miss them, but watch out for the queues.

For those with a head for heights, climb the Dome, but I warn you, the gallery up there is narrow and the balustrade low. The Dome was completed by Brunelleschi in 1434 – and for creating such a marvellous structure, he was accorded a singular honour, for he is one of the few Florentines to be buried in the cathedral.
The Campanile, nearly three hundred feet high, towers overhead, dwarfed only by the very top of the Dome itself. Designed by the artist Giotto, it was built between 1334 and 1459 and is one of the very greatest examples of Gothic art. It is also remarkable because its designer was an artist, and not an architect or engineer!
In its shadow is the Baptistry. At one time it was thought that this had been converted from the Temple of Mars, but current opinion has it dating from the 10th or 11th century, becoming the Baptistry, or Cathedral, of St. John in 1228. Romanesque in style, the interior is paved with 13th and 14th century mosaics. Its three doors are magnificent, one by Andrea da Pontedera and the others by Lorenzo Ghiberti, who took 27 years to create these masterpieces in bronze: they feature scenes from the Old Testament, and are so beautiful that Michelangelo dubbed them "the gates of paradise".

From Piazza del Duomo head northwards along Via Ricasoli, and in two blocks you'll reach the Galleria del Accademia. Founded in 1784 by Grand Duke Pietro Leopold of Lorraine who wanted to provide a place where students could study examples of art from all the periods, it is today most famous as the home of Michelangelo's 'David', as I said earlier, relocated from the Piazza della Signora for its safety. In the summer months you can expect long queues here as well, for everyone wants to see the original. Paintings on display include works by Botticelli and others.

If you now head back towards the Cathedral but instead of using the Via Ricasoli you use the road to its right, the Via Cavour, in the space of just one block you'll reach Palazzo Medici Ricardi. Cosimo the elder built this between 1444 and 1464. Conservative in appearance on the outside, it is less so inside for upstairs is the Medici Chapel, where the family could pray in surroundings so luxurious that they've been described as 'heavenly'. Paintings of the Medici themselves grace the walls, and there is a painted ceiling glorifying the family.

You are now very close to another great place of worship, San Lorenzo, the Medici parish church: early Christian in style, it is as large and as grand as many of its Gothic neighbours and is the last resting place of several of the Medicis: Cosimo is buried in front of the main altar, whilst others of the family are interred in and near the Sacristy. The church was built by Brunelleschi, but by the time of his death it was still incomplete so the façade was never built although Michelangelo did design one, and a model of this in wood can be seen in Casa Buonarroti, the Michelangelo Museum, which stands just to the north of Santa Croce. If you'd like to visit this, then as you head back towards your coach, on reaching Piazza Santa Croce turn left into a street called Via Giuseppe Verdi. Walk for one block, turn right along Via Ghibellina and in a short distance the Michelangelo Museum is on your left. It is worth visiting, for more of his works are on display here, including his 'Madonna of the Stair', and the 'Battle of the Centaurs' – as well as that model of San Lorenzo, of course!

Leaving the Museum, retrace your steps to Santa Croce, and you are then ten minutes away from your coach, your all-too-brief visit to this magnificent place all but over.

Market lovers would like to know that there are a couple of good markets – I've already mentioned Mercato Nuovo – the 'Straw Market' – home to that bronze boar and very close to the Piazza della Republica. The central market, Mercato Centrale, lies just to the north of San Lorenzo, and in both of them you'll find leather goods, souvenirs, silk ties and scarves and all manner of goodies that testify to the fact that Florence is a pretty chic place – remember my early comments?

Shopping is good in the area around Piazza della Republica and the Via Roma, and there are hundreds of restaurants and cafes all waiting to relieve you of a few Euros: especially noteworthy are those that have pavement tables around Piazza della Signoria. Sit there and enjoy a coffee while you gaze at the world which is, in turn, gazing at the replica of David and at the wonders of the Loggia dei Lanzi.

Early on in this chapter I said that a large proportion of the world's best artworks are to be found in Florence. In all likelihood you'll only be here for six or seven hours, so you'll have to be very selective – it simply is not possible for you to see everything. There are dozens of other museums, galleries, churches, palaces and fountains. If I have omitted something in which you are particularly interested, please accept my apologies – any number of very detailed and comprehensive guides exist, and in all probability you'll find two or three in the library on board.

Florence is a wonderful city but now, sadly, you must leave because Pisa and a few other Tuscan beauties beckon!

Without a shadow of doubt you will be offered an excursion to Pisa, that second remarkable Tuscan city whose 'Leaning Tower' is recognised throughout the world. I've already explained that you can get there under your own steam by train (or taxi) from Livorno, and I've said that a tour or two will be offered in combination with Florence: for the sake of this discussion, then, I'm going to assume that you'll take a similar 'Pisa on your Own' excursion, or that you'll opt for independence and take that twelve mile train ride from Livorno, and for the sake of clarity I'll use the Railway Station as a starting point because a coach could drop you off at any one of two or three different sites and I don't want to confuse you. You're in for a treat!

Pisa is another hugely historic place that claims to have been founded by the Greeks even though most historians dispute this. Whatever its early origins, by the 11th century it had established a lucrative little empire embracing Corsica, Sardinia, other Mediterranean islands and parts of North Africa. In 1135 it captured Amalfi, and it was Pisa's archbishop who led the entire Christian fleet in support of the Christian Knights of the First Crusade – an event that was fortuitous for the Pisans who played a canny card in their dealings with their Arab protagonists: they learned from them and imported much of their science and know-how.

In time, the city developed a reputation for its scholastic traditions and Arabic numerals were introduced to Europe by a Pisan mathematician, a man called Leonardo Fibinacci and in the 1600s when Galileo Galilei rose to fame the city could claim him as one of its sons.

Despite all this, Pisa started to experience decline from about 1284, when its navy was decimated by Genoa, the rapidly expanding, opportunistic, city-state that lies but a short distance up the coast. Pisa's hold on its trade routes was lost and its influence in the region dwindled. Then its harbour silted up and its fate seemed inevitable – until the Medicis of Florence decided to move their university here, a move that probably enabled the city to survive. Most of the best known of Pisa's sights lie in the Campo dei Miracoli, the Field of Miracles, so called because of the enormously ambitious building programme that commenced with the Cathedral and went on to include the Baptistry, the Camposanto and the Leaning Tower, each hugely impressive in its own right, and each a magnet for today's tourists.

The Station, our starting point, lies on the southern side of the city, about a mile and a half from the Field of Miracles – if you feel energetic, you can hire a bicycle nearby and save yourself a walk, or take a taxi. Your route will take you through the centre, past the Botanical Gardens to Piazza dei Miracoli, which runs adjacent to the Field.

The Cathedral, the oldest building in the complex, was started in around 1064 and is regarded as one of the finest Pisan-Romanesque buildings in Tuscany. It has a wonderful, creamy white, tiered façade and the Biblical scenes on the central brass doors were cast by Bonnano Pisano. The inside is cavernous, dark and rather austere, but the baptismal font is worth seeing, and the pulpit, by Giovanni Pisano, is a masterpiece. Next to it is a brass lamp that supposedly belonged to Galileo and tradition would have it that scientist used the lamp in his experiments with movement. Elsewhere in the building are paintings, frescoes and mosaics, perhaps the most notable of which is in the apse, 'Christ in Majesty'.

The Baptistry, the biggest of its kind in Italy, dates from 1153, is of white marble and circular in form: its Gothic crown of gables and pinnacles reaches a height of a hundred and seventy nine feet. The marble font inside, the work of Guido Bigarelli, dates back to 1246 and the pulpit by Nicola Pisano is magnificent. The building is famed for its acoustics and is a truly beautiful place to visit. But the universal symbol of the city is undoubtedly The Campanile or Bell Tower – the so-called 'Leaning Tower of Pisa' – work on which started in 1173 and ended in 1350. It is now thought that the foundations on the southern side subsided during construction, although there has long been a school of thought, suggested by a group of architects who measured the stones in the 19th century, that the lean was quite deliberate: some even suggest that Galileo used the tower for his experiments with gravity! Whatever the truth, the fact is that it lies about sixteen feet out of true. Engineers have installed steel cables and 100 tons of lead to stabilise the structure and today the angle of lean is roughly the same as it was in 1810. Closed during these works, the building is once again open to a public clamouring to get in, so do be prepared to queue.

The fourth constituent of the Field of Miracles is the cemetery, or Camposanto. A long, rectangular building of marble arcades, it dates from 1278 when its creator, Giovanni de Simone, started working on the site. The bombers of World War II caused massive damage, destroying a great deal including many of its magnificent frescoes, but traces of one, 'The Triumph of Death', can still be seen. Some of the soil enclosed by the walls is supposedly from the Holy Land.

Apart from the Field of Miracles the town has a number of other attractions, including more churches, pleasant buildings and attractive squares. I've already mentioned the Botanical Gardens: pause by these as you pass for they are amongst the oldest of their type in Europe. Don't miss the historic town centre with the Palazzo dell'Orologio (1607), the old quays and houses along the Arno, and the Palazzo Toscanelli, where Byron lived during his time here, which is down by the river. The Museo Nazionale di San Matteo, on the northern river bank exhibits a good range of Pisan and Florentine art and is worth a visit. Compared to Florence, you'll find the town quiet but there is fair bit to see for it is an important place with a university and a vibrant industrial and commercial life.

In this chapter I've tried to convey something of the beauty of Florence and Pisa, and you've probably guessed that I love them both. But, as I said right at the beginning of the chapter, the whole of this region is glorious and if you've been to these two jewels before and your cruise is offering an excursion or two into the crown itself, do consider them!

For example, there may be one heading for San Gimignano, another to Volterra, or even a third to Puccini's Villa at Lake Massaciuccoli. Go for one of them, for you will not only encounter more of that very special Tuscan countryside en route, but will find that San Gimignano and Volterra are charming and a visit to Puccini's lakeside retreat will surely help you to better understand where the composer got his inspiration!

San Gimignano is a medieval town, boasting no less than thirteen towers built by its noble families during the 12th and 13th centuries. Standing astride the pilgrim route from northern Europe to Rome, it enjoyed enormous prosperity in the middle ages until it was devasted by the Plague in 1348. The pilgrim route was diverted, and the town's wealth migrated with it. Today, it is a delightful place to visit, although only one of its towers, called Torre Grossa, is open to the public. Town, walls, cobbled streets, plenty of works of art, good shops and the odd restaurant or two all add up to a great atmosphere. There is a 12th century Romanesque Cathedral, the Collegiata, which is home to a number of beautiful frescoes including one dating from 1367 called 'The Creation'. A painting called 'The Annunciation' by Ghirlandio can be seen in a courtyard loggia near the church, and the council chamber of the Palazzo del Popolo is worth looking at. If time permits, take the opportunity to sit in the sunshine and sample a drop or two of the local Vernaccio wine!

Volterra is an Etruscan town situated on a high plateau. In places you can see remnants of the surrounding Etruscan walls, and its museum, the Museo Guarnacci, is home to one of the best collection of Etruscan artefacts anywhere in the country. Another Pisan-Romanesque Cathedral stands on the Piazza San Giovanni and there is a good art gallery, the Pinacoteca e Museo Civico with some good paintings by several Florentine artists including a work by Rosso Fiorentino called 'The Deposition'.

Finally for this chapter I'll touch on Lake Massaciuccoli, site of that lakeside retreat that spawned the beautiful works of Giacomo Puccini who was born in Lucca in 1858 and lived on the shores of this lake until his death in 1924. The lake lies to the south of Viareggio, and to reach it you drive through tall pine forests which border its shores. A nature reserve, your tour is likely to include a boat trip, during which you'll glide on the placid waters and sip a glass or two of wine whilst listening to the strains of 'Tosca' and you'll be transported back in time – and when you get there be glad you're not a duck, for Puccini's other great love was duck shooting!

You'll be taken next to the Villa itself, the Torre de Lago, wherein you'll see Puccini's piano and several other artefacts that'll remind you of his genius. You'll also be shown his hunting rifle!

Alas, we come to the end of our Tuscan dream. In conclusion, a few practicalities for you. The currency is still the Euro; please remember to wear modest dress for churches and cathedrals – bare shoulders and shorts are not acceptable; if you've taken a transfer coach from Livorno to either Florence or Pisa, don't be late re-joining it for your return journey – the driver will not wait and a taxi from Florence costs about £100! Remember, too, about taking care with the timing of independent journeys: missing your ship will traumatise you!

Whatever you do during your stay in Livorno, have a fabulous time – I know you will.

NAPLES
Italy

Remember the Back Streets!

The Bay of Naples

Castel Nuovo

Piazza Plebiscito

The Royal Palace

Cathedral

Museum of San Martino

Archaeological Museum

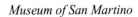

NAPLES, Italy
Remember the back streets....?

If Calabria is the 'toe' of Italy, then Campania is its shin: if the country was wearing a high-heeled anklestrap shoe, then the strap would pass right through Naples, ancient capital of the region and our next port of call.

Sprawling around the beautiful Bay of Naples the city is huge, noisy and chaotic and suffers from unenviable unemployment that promotes a high level of crime. Don't take your valuables ashore here and if you're given to wearing designer watches and jewellery, leave them on board! Street vendors will tempt you with all manner of goodies, from binoculars to video cameras – but do be careful! A very experienced seafaring friend of mine was delighted to find a state-of-the art video camera on sale on a street corner, for about a third of its usual price. He haggled successfully, knocking the price down to a cool two hundred euros, paid, and was absolutely delighted when the smiling Neapolitan handed him a brand new, cellophane wrapped box – not for him the shop-soiled display one. Clutching his treasure he rushed back to the ship, changed into uniform and went on duty, leaving his still wrapped purchase in his cabin. It was only when he came off watch, the ship now far down the coast, that he settled down to examine his camera – and discovered that he had paid two hundred Euros for a couple of old bricks. But they were beautifully presented. Be warned!

It was Peter Sarsted who penned the immortal words "Oh, remember the back streets of Naples, two children dressed only in rags...", – words which always conjure up for me visions of Sophia Loren as an urchin child in those streets (so they say) although hard to imagine her there today! For the back streets are ancient, the crumbling plaster of their houses in need of far more than a lick of paint – but they are fascinating for all that and so crowded. Here, even the newest of cars bear the scars of many encounters with others, for Neapolitan drivers always seem to be hell bent upon making it through the narrowest of gaps before the other guy.

The Bay of Naples is bounded by Vesuvius, in the shadow of which lie Herculaneum and Pompeii, both destroyed by the volcano, and the islands of Capri, Ischia and Procida – but it is Napleas that has been beautifully described as having a 'rude ebullience', and for all its squalor and poverty it can be a captivating place. Let's have a look at it.

The port is a busy one – commercial and naval quays, ship repair yards, bustling ferries of all shapes and sizes vie with lay-up berths where the ships of bankrupt owners lie awaiting their fate and a very large cruise terminal. Disembarking, you'll find yourself in a cavernous building where the souvenir shops, news stalls, tourist information points and post offices all seem a little lost and your footfalls echo on marble stairs.

In front of the building you'll emerge onto a tarmac concourse where multitudes of taxis, coaches and people scurry in a seemingly never ending stream towards the dock gates, a couple of hundred yards distant. Follow them and you'll find yourself on an extremely busy, multi-lane street called Via Cristoforo Colombo (haven't we heard that name before in these chapters?) along which the traffic roars, horns blaring, absolutely indifferent to you, a mere pedestrian. Do NOT attempt to cross except at the clearly marked, controlled, crossings!

By way of orientation: walk straight ahead having crossed Via Cristoforo Colombo, keeping the massive castle, Castel Nuovo, on your left and in a matter of a hundred yards or so you'll reach Piazza Municipio, a large oblong square that forms the hub of this part of the city. Municipio is bounded to your right by the commercial district which stretches into the exhaust fume laden distance, all the way to the National Archaeological Museum in the north and Castel Capuano and the city gates of the same name in the north east: the Duomo, (Cathedral), lies between them. Straight ahead of you, to the west, lies the Quartieri Spagnoli (Spanish Quarter), whilst on your left is Castel Nuovo and beyond it the Royal Palace (Palazzo Real) and another enormous square called Piazza del Plebiscito. Nearer at hand is the Via San Carlo with the Theatre of the same name on its left hand side and on its right the magnificent, if a little tired, glass-roofed arcade called the Galleria Umberto. All of these are within easy walking distance, and all are worth seeing.

The Castel Nuovo, built between 1279 and 1282 for Charles of Anjou is also referred to as Chateau d'Anjou for it was the principal residence of the Angevin kings who ruled here until the arrival of the Aragonese in 1443. In a rather unusual application of an age old concept, they incorporated a impressive triumphal arch over the castle's entrance in 1454 to commemorate their achievements. In 1486 Ferdinand of Aragon squashed a major uprising here, another event in the long and chequered history of the castle. Today, part of the building is devoted to the city's Civic Museum, so if you want to know more about the history of the Castle and the city go inside and browse among the exhibits.

Heading up Via San Carlo, Italy's oldest and largest opera house, Teatro San Carlo is on your left. Originally built in 1737 for Charles of Bourbon, it was later remodelled with a particularly luxurious auditorium that became the envy of many similar establishments in other parts of Europe. Opposite is one of the entrances to the Galleria Umberto, the enormous glass covered arcade that was built in 1887 as a focal point for fashionable Neapolitans. Today the Galleria is a little shabby, but is still home to some rather smart shops, coffee houses and the like, and as you walk by you'll have little difficulty imagining how grand it all must have been in its heyday.

The western frontage of the Galleria is on the Via Toledo, also known as Via Roma, and this major highway trends north all the way to the National Archaeological Museum – too far away to reach comfortably on foot so better left until later.

For the moment, cross Via San Carlo heading south and you'll have the Royal Palace on your left, and that very large square, Piazza del Plebiscito, right ahead. Traffic has been banned from this and its enormous colonnades flank the portals of a church called San Francisco di Paola, its portals reminiscent of Rome's Pantheon. Opposite stands the Royal Palace with its façade adorned with statues representing all the dynasties of Naples. A good looking building, it was originally built for the Viceroys of Spain in 1600 and enlarged by some of its later residents. Today it is home to the Biblioteca Nazionale and many of its rooms are filled with fine paintings, tapestries and furniture. There is an attractive area of gardens lying behind the Palace and you can stroll through these on your way back to the Piazza Municipio, thereby avoiding the traffic on Via San Carlo.

But before you re-trace your steps, take a wander into the Spanish Quarter which is just across Via Toledo and a stone's throw from Galleria Umberto. I know that it will not be to everyone's taste, but it is quintessentially Naples and the part of the city that Peter Sarsted was thinking of when he wrote that song, so clearly dedicated to Ms. Loren. The Quarter is one of the city's most densely populated areas, its labyrinthine maze of tiny narrow streets festooned with washing and badly dented cars, its pavements awash with litter, its air thick with the smells of garlic and unwashed socks. But it is alive and intriguing – come here by day by all means, perhaps better to avoid it at night, when its alleyways become rather more sinister and intimidating.

Walking through this maze one day, Rosie (my wife), and I chanced upon a fruit seller, his baskets of fresh figs spilling in warm, green, abundance onto the pavement. The temptation was too much, and for a euro or two we hurried away, our purchase clutched protectively to our bosom. Around the next corner and out of sight of the fruit seller we set to and devoured the whole lot – sweet, warm, heaven – with abandon. True to their promise, they worked quickly and we were forced to leg it across that huge coach park outside the terminal building and back to the ship before being engulfed in personal calamities at least as mighty as those which befell Pompeii and Herculaneum. So, be warned – the figs are potent!

I said that the Cathedral and one or two of the other tourist sites are out of walking reach – it is possible to walk, of course, but I'm talking of a mile or two rather than a couple of hundred yards, so you may consider a cab if you're doing Naples independently.

The Cathedral of San Gennaro stands on the Via Duomo in the northern part of the city quite close to the Capuana Gates and the central station. Built between the late 13th and early 14th centuries, it has a much later façade which dates from the 19th. The Cathedral is named after the city's patron saint, Saint Gennaro, martyred in 305AD. His head is kept in a gilt bust, his congealed blood in a couple of phials and the rest of his body in a 16th century tomb called the Cappella Carafa. A rather revolting tradition has it that the blood miraculously liquefies three times each year and that, should it fail to do so, the city will run into a period of ill fortune. The Cathedral is home to a number of monuments to Naples' former rulers and there are one or two fine paintings by the likes of Domenichino.

Eastwards of the Cathedral and a short distance away is Castel Capuano, a Norman palace that became the Courts of Justice in 1540 and which still functions as a courthouse. The nearby Porta Capuano, or Capua Gate, is worth seeing for it is a Renaissance gateway in the Florentine tradition.

Reach this far, and you've reached the central station. If you are intending to visit Herculaneum, Pompeii and Sorrento on your own, then you can catch a train from here. The trains are painless, inexpensive and regular and the journey to Sorrento (the furthest of the three) takes about an hour. But the same word of caution applies: do plan your journeys carefully for the next port on our itinerary, Corfu, is a long swim! Also, do make sure you recognise a few landmarks on your outward journey: on one memorable occasion after a pleasant lunch in Sorrento where the wine flowed quite freely, Rosie and I caught the train back to Naples. Arriving at a station whose sign read 'NAPOLI' I insisted that this was our destination and proceeded to get off the train. In her wisdom, she insisted that it was not and during the ensuing argument the automatic doors closed, leaving me on the platform with all the money, the tickets and our all-important Boarding Cards, and Rosie on the train – with nothing. Try as I might I couldn't open the doors and, in danger of falling ignominiously off the end of the platform, I had to let it go. The train went and my wife went with it. Believing that I was now on the platform of Naples Station, I concluded that the train was now heading for Milan or somewhere equally inaccessible and that the best thing that I could do was get back to the ship there to await the return (or not, as the case may be), of my errant wife. I started to walk and after about four miles the realisation dawned – the station had not been NAPOLI CENTRALE but NAPOLI (Suburb), some remote corner on the far distant periphery of the city, in the middle of nowhere. The ship was due to sail in about an hour and I was left with no alternative and started running. Eventually arriving at the gangway, considerably the worse for wear – and thinner – the security people confirmed that my wife had not (miraculously) returned and my plight deepened: remember, that she had nothing with her, not even the means to get off whatever platform she was destined to arrive at. I dreamed, momentarily and regretfully, about the security of the ship's tours, and then ventured out onto the chaos of Via Cristoforo Colombo, there to plead with the deities – or anyone – for Rosie's safe return. To cut a long and painful story short, she made it in the nick of time and I found her, tearfully pleading with an irate taxi driver who could see, quite correctly, no prospect of payment. I paid and we made it back on board as the lines were let go, the deep throated rumble of the ship's whistle signalling our departure. My feet were the size of water melons, my nerves shot to pieces, and my marriage in jeopardy. Do check your journeys carefully, because even the Destination Lecturer, supposedly the font of all wisdom, can get it badly wrong!

Still in the northern part of the city but on its opposite side stands the National Archaeological Museum (Museo Archeologico Nazionale), one of the most important of its kind in the world. The building in which it is housed started life in the late 16th century as the barracks for the Royal cavalry, then in the 17th it became the home of the city's univerisity. In 1777 the university was moved elsewhere and the building was adapted to house a museum. It was badly damaged by an earthquake in 1980 and restoration is still in progress. Notable works on display include a 1st century BC bronze bust, thought to be of Seneca the Elder, a wine vessel called 'The Blue Vase' that was found in a Pompeii tomb, the Farnese Bull, a very large sculptural group that was excavated from the Baths of Caracalla in Rome and the Farnese Hercules, a copy of a piece by Lysippius. In a room called The Secret Cabinet can be seen erotic works that were originally in Pompeii and Herculaneum – there is nothing new under the sun! Look out, too, for a mosaic from Pompeii showing Alexander the Great defeating Darius III, Persian Emperor of 333BC.

Once again, we're talking here of a large city with much to see. But, by now you know that you have to be selective and if you manage to see some of the sights that I've told you about, you'll have done well. As usual, I'll now take you further afield, outside the city limits and the ship's excursions are a good starting point.

You will most certainly be offered a tour to Pompeii, since this is one of the biggest tourist attractions, not only in Campania but in all of Italy. I've already told you how to get here independently – but, if you choose to do this, you won't have the benefit of a guide, you'll likely have to queue to get in and you'll certainly have to make your way to the site from the railway station. So, the best option is to avail yourself of the tour – you'll reach the ancient city painlessly, and will be shown everything so that when you get back to the ship, you'll know so much more about it all.

Vesuvius erupted with cataclysmic consequences for the thriving city of Pompeii in August, 79AD. About two thousand of the city's total population of twenty odd thousand died, engulfed in a sea of ash and pumice which covered their ancient Greco-Roman home to a depth of about twenty feet. Apart from efficiently extinguishing a great deal of life here, the strata of volcanic matter effectively preserved the city, so that today's visitor can experience the reality of those far off days, sometimes in macabre detail. The extraordinary preservation has given the modern world a unique insight into the daily lives of the people of that age and many of Pompeii's artefacts are safely housed in the National Museum of Archaeology in Naples: I've already suggested in this chapter that you go there and see them for yourselves.

The most impressive part of Pompeii is the western sector accessed by the Porta Marina entrance at the southwestern edge of the town. Here you'll be shown several intact Roman ruins as well as the remains of the forum, or principal market place.

An important street was the Via dell Abbondanza, one time home to many of its pubs and restaurants. Towards the western end of this stands the Teatro Grande, its serried ranks of seats almost as they were nineteen hundred and twenty odd years ago when it was a centre of entertainment. Your guide will take you to the House of Vettii, one of Pompeii's finest: Its owners were not aristocrats but freed former slaves who made their pile as traders and lavished their home with evidence of their success. The walls of the villa are covered with frescoes – in the dining room, there is a frieze of a cupids' chariot race that is quite astonishing – and the pots and pans in the nearby kitchen all look poised for the preparation of lunch! The house incorporates an internal garden, a Greek idea enthusiastically adopted in this instance by Romans.

When I was talking about the Archaeological Museum in Naples I mentioned a mosaic of Alexander the Great – this was found in the House of the Faun, next on your probable agenda. The house was named after a bronze statuette that was the pride and joy of its owner, a man called Casii. On your tour you'll see the local flour mill and bakehouse from which petrified loaves of bread were excavated, and then, on the floor of another house, you'll smile at a mosaic warning intruders to Beware of the Dog – Cave Canem! – and I'm sure the dog in the picture is a Rottweiler!

Countless wagon wheels have deeply rutted several of Pompeii's roads and the local council seem to have developed a unique idea for their repair – they simply laid stepping stones over them! (our local council back home should think on – rather stones like these than the holes which mar our roads).

Pompeii is a truly remarkable place and a poignant reminder of how catastrophe can strike in one fleeting, dreadful, moment.

Where ash and the detritus of explosion engulfed this town, nearby Herculaneum (Ercolano, in Italian) was swamped by a sea of mud, which evidently was kinder (and slower) in its advance for it is thought that few, if any, of Herculaneum's residents perished, having had, it seems, more time to flee the onslaught. The town was originally named Herakleia after its patron Hercules and perhaps it was the strength that he endowed that enabled many of the buildings to withstand inundation. Visit the town today, and you can see many of them, more or less in their original condition.

Enough of cataclysm, death and destruction! The Bay of Naples has much beauty as well as its teeming city, brooding volcano and ancient ruins: it is home to Capri, Ischia, Procida and Sorrento, and around the next cape lies what must be one of the most beautiful coastlines anywhere in the world – the coast of Amalfi.

Your ship will certainly be offering tours to one or more of these delights but again, for the independently minded among you there is yet another alternative to the tour or train.

Stepping out of the Cruise Terminal onto that massive concourse, if you head slightly to your left rather than straight ahead for the dock gates you'll come upon the ferry port, and ferries leave from here for Sorrento, Capri and points further south. They sail punctually, inexpensively and with a frequency that would be the envy of Connex South Central and you can buy your ticket from the kiosks that line the landward side of the ferry building then join your boat for the journey across the Bay. Many of the ferries are fast hydrofoils which bounce about in any sort of sea, are more akin to an aircraft than a boat inside and can get hot, smelly and claustrophobic. Nevertheless, they get you there in pretty short order and are certainly a lot faster than anything else.

The Sorrento peninsular lies between the Bay of Naples and the Bay of Salerno and has been inhabited since Neolithic times. Sorrento itself is thirty miles south of Naples and is much sought after by both visitors and native Italians, offering a delightful combination of land- and seascapes, all bathed beneath glorious Mediterranean skies.

Invoking Greek mythology, the Romans named this as the legendary abode of the Sirens – those wicked mermaids who used to lure seamen to their deaths with their sweet songs. Homer, in his Odyssey, told of Ulysses resisting their call by having himself lashed to the mast – hopefully you won't have to go to the same lengths, but it is a lovely place!

Greek colonists first settled these coasts between the 6th and 8th centuries, and Sorrento was probably colonised at around the same time as Naples which was known to the Greeks as Neapolis, or New Town. With the help of the nearby Sicilians, the locals resisted an Etruscan attempt at take-over, only to face another threat by other fierce intruders soon after. Lasting peace in the area was only established by the Romans, and the town really began to flourish when wealthy Romans built their holiday villas here some two thousand years ago.

High on the cliffs overlooking the Bays of Naples and Salerno, the town has been sending out its own siren call ever since, luring visitors from far and near. Despite this it is a fact that after the demise of the Roman Empire there followed centuries of changing fortunes, and often Sorrento's inhabitants suffered at the hands of greedy overlords – but thankfully they never spoiled the scenery. Testament to its enduring beauty is the fact that people like Wagner, Nietzsche and Gorky lived and worked here and Ibsen wrote "The Ghosts" whilst under the influence of the haunted quality of the town at night, its dimly but artistically lit environs barely visible in the depths of its gorges.

Modernisation came with Napoleon, and the 19th century saw great strides in communications, although the terrain necessitates narrow twisting roads that frequently cause heavy traffic congestion and the odd bout of car sickness. The economy today is boosted by tourism, but depends too on olives and vineyards, fruit and nut groves, large citrus plantations and fishing.

Sorrento stands on a terrace of rock with a sheer drop from the cliffs to the sea, although many of the places of interest in the town stand close together near Piazza Tasso, named after the town's most famous poet whose life spanned the second half of the 16th century. Tasso had great influence on literature in this period, his most famous work being "Jerusalem Delivered". He was buried in the church which stands on the side of the 9th century square of San Antonio.

Main Street is called Corso Italia and on this you'll find the Cathedral. Rebuilt in the 15th century it has a mock Gothic facade and houses traditional Italian handicrafts in its Bishop's Throne and Choir Stalls. The nearby Chiesa de San Francisco has a 14th century cloister, delicate archways and a pretty garden of flowering vines and museum lovers will want to visit the Museo Correale di Terranova, the former palace and home of the Correale family. As you would expect, the museum has fine displays of ancient statues, antiques and Italian art.

The coast from Sorrento onwards, called Costiera Amalfitana or the Amalfi Coast, is stunning: as I said earlier, it has got to be one of the most beautful coastlines in the world. Catch a bus to Positano from Sorrento if there is no tour on offer – but be prepared for some hair-raising hairpin bends and one or two places where you will swear that your coach will never make it and that your days are destined to end on the rocks, seemingly thousands of feet below: close your eyes and think of England and as you round that dreaded bend and another vista opens up before you, you really will be glad that you came – I promise!

Positano village tumbles down its hillside to the sea: make your way to the waterfront and you'll probably trip over a 'celebrity' or two, for this undoubtedly is home to the holidaying jet set. (By the way, if one journey on that bus is enough, you can actually catch a ferry from here to Capri, and thence back to Naples). Amalfi is next down the coast but as it is just that much further it really falls outside the scope of this book: suffice to say that all of this coastline is superb and if you ever contemplate a non-cruising holiday (heaven forbid!), you might like to remember this and return when you've got a little more time.

Backtracking, I'll tell you something of Capri. The Romans found this too, and they loved it and made it a resort for emperors. Since then it has been, variously, a place of exile, a playground for the wealthy and a retreat for expatriates. It was also, of course, the place that inspired that romantic songwriter to pen that immortal ode to his lady. Today it is always thronged with tourists and it seems that its traders, hoteliers, restauranteurs (and probably even its shepherds) have never learned the meaning of a 'low season' and are intimately acquainted with the art of overcharging. But, it is beautiful and there is much to see. The principal town is Capri and the port is Marina Grande, always clogged with yachts, ferries, pleasure craft and beautiful people, all overlooked by pretty houses that tower over the harbour in colourful profusion. The second town is Anacapri and this too is thronged, as is the Blue Grotto and the Villa Jovis, mountain retreat from which Tiberius ruled the Roman Empire.

On occasion, I've heard the odd passenger ask why Naples was included on the itinerary, for at first glance it does seem to be just another big, sprawling, and, in part ugly, city. But it is not, as I hope I've shown.

Whether you've decided to stay in Naples, or wonder at the destruction of ancient Pompeii, or take that bus ride to Positano or admire the views from Capri, I hope that you've enjoyed your time here.

Arrivederci!

SICILY
AND THE STRAITS OF MESSINA

If Corfu is your next port of call as it is in this book, you'll have a day at sea in which to recover from all the sightseeing. Sailing almost due south you'll reach the Aeolian Islands (Isole Eolie). Depending on the timing of your passage, it is worth being on deck to see the island of Stromboli, a volcano that is always in eruption. It is quite docile, it must be said, but worth seeing, especially if you've never seen an erupting volcano before. It's best seen in the dark when the glow of the cone is more impressive than the smoke which is the only evidence of activity by day. Amazingly, there is a town on its lower slopes where the population goes about its business unconcernedly and ferries run to and fro – I wonder how many of their passengers are tourists! The largest of the Aeolian group is Lipari, a few miles to the south and nearer to the coast of Sicily.

Stromboli lies about an hour's steaming from the Straits of Messina which are worth staying on deck to see, for they are impressive. At their narrowest point, very close to the northern entrance, they are but a mile and a half wide and the sea eddies thorough the gap between the island and the mainland: the whirlpools of Scylla and Charibdis of mythology were located here, and in fact there is a tiny town called Scilla on the Italian side that is named after them. Approaching, the dominant features are the massive electricity pylons on either side of the straits – pylons that used to carry the cables which brought power to the island but which are defunct now having been replaced by undersea cables: it is said that they are too expensive to remove so they stand sentinel over the Straits. The mainland shoreline here is steep, with terraced hillsides, whilst at this point the Sicilian one here is flat with a little town nestling in the shadow of the lighthouse on the point. Pilotage through the straits is mandatory, and you'll see the pilot arrive when still about half a mile from the entrance. Although navigating the straits is not difficult, local knowledge of those eddies and current flow is necessary, and these are busy waters – not only with transit traffic but also with a host of local ferries plying their route between the Italian towns of Reggio di Calabria or San Giovanni and Messina.

Sweeping through the straits, the land on both sides becomes more densely built up as your ship makes its way south and eastwards: Messina and its suburbs lie to starboard, and San Giovanni to port. If the day is clear, you'll see the brooding mass of Etna, towering over all, in the far distance to starboard.

Leaving Messina astern watch for the beautiful town of Taormina on its hillside to starboard. Then we sail on, with the land on both sides receding into the distance. The Adriatic lies ahead.

CORFU
Greece

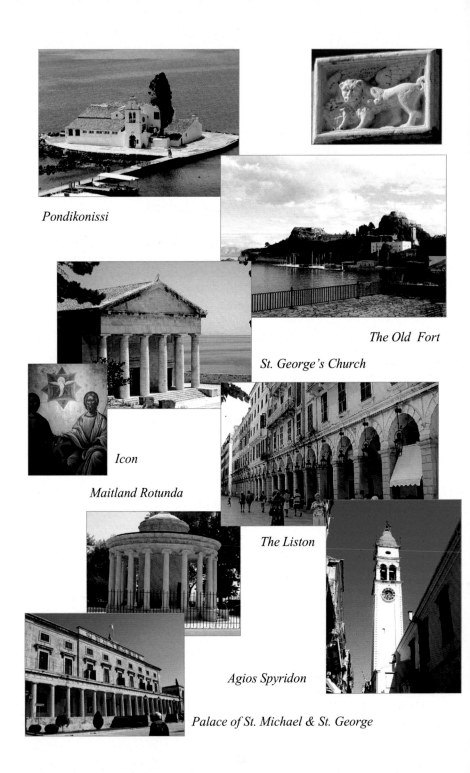

Pondikonissi

The Old Fort

St. George's Church

Icon

Maitland Rotunda

The Liston

Agios Spyridon

Palace of St. Michael & St. George

CORFU
Odysseus' nemesis?

The second largest of the Ionian Islands with a land area of about 220 square miles, Corfu is the westernmost part of Greece and is separated from the coast of Albania by a stretch of water about a mile and a half wide. Looking at a map you'll see that it is elongated in shape: the northern part is the most mountainous, with the highest peak, Mount Pantokrator, rising majestically 3,000 feet above the sea.

Corfu Town lies about half way up the east coast, with the mainland shore almost directly opposite – at this point, Greece lies about ten miles distant with the narrowest part of the strait separating Corfu from Albania a little further to the north.

The island's strategic geographical position has guaranteed the envious gaze of many an aggressor over the centuries – the Byzantines, the Venetians and the Ottoman Turks among them. The shoreline is very varied, with much of the west coast mountainous and rocky, the northern and eastern more gently sloping. It is a beautiful place, with wooded offshore islets adding much to its appeal and serenity. But by no means has it always been peaceful and serene. According to Homer, it was once inhabited by a prosperous and happy people, the Phaecians, a race who loved music and dancing, were much beloved by the gods and had, as their first king, Nausithoos, son of Poseidon. Originally they had lived in a place called Hypereia, but were forced to flee it because of relentless harassment on the part of their neighbours and they ended up here on Corfu which was, for them, an island at the end of the world where they hoped that they would be able to settle in peace.

They built for themselves a fine city with bronze walls and golden portals, and a fabulous palace surrounded by royal estates which were rich in fruit trees and vines: it was a land of enchantment. The Phaecians were fine seafarers with ships possessed of magical powers of navigation, and legends abound of them coming to the aid of less capable mariners who found themselves in trouble on these shores. One such castaway was Odysseus and the tale is that he hauled himself ashore from shipwreck and fell asleep amongst the bushes of the shoreline, where he was found by a beautiful princess called Nausikaa. She was entranced by him and became so concerned about his plight that she persuaded him to present himself to her mother Queen Arete, telling him that, if he succeeded in gaining the Queen's sympathy she would for a certainty arrange for him to return to his homeland without further ado. He did, and she did, and the Phaeacians loaded up a ship with all manner of goodies to help him on his journey. But in so doing they incurred Poseidon's wrath, and he struck Odysseus's ship with the palm of his hand and turned it into stone – and many is the rock island off the coast that claims to be that ship!

Scholars have tried in vain to place the Phaeacian capital in various different parts of the island, but have never found any archaeological evidence so your guess as to its whereabouts is as good as mine. Archaeological finds have, however, pointed to habitation during the Palaeolithic era, when it is thought that the island adjoined the mainland, and important Neolothic and Bronze Age settlements have been unearthed on the west coast. The earliest known Greek settlement dates from about the 8th century BC and colonists from Corinth settled here in 734BC.

Trading successfully with other cities along the Adriatic coast, the island became prosperous during the 6th and 5th centuries BC, but a series of misfortunes led to a quite dramatic decline so that by the end of the 4th century its people were in trouble. Plundered by Illyrian forces, they were obliged to surrender to the Illyrian Queen Teuta in 229BC, and she appointed a man called Demetrios Pharios as Governor: he betrayed her and handed the island over to the Romans, who thus gained their first Greek dependency without having to lift a finger.

Christianity arrived here thanks to the evangelising of Jason and Sosipater, two disciples of Christ's apostle Paul then, when Emperor Diocletian divided the Roman empire into east and west, Corfu fell into the eastern half which later became Byzantine. The island continued to suffer at the hands of maurauders – the Vandals, the Goths and the Saracens and it was during this period that the Old Fort, which to our day dominates the modern town, was built .

The Fourth Crusade of 1204, which heralded the sack of Constantinople and the division amongst the Crusaders of much of the Byzantine Empire saw Corfu pass to the Venetians, who promptly divided the island into ten fiefs, giving one to each of ten Venetian Noblemen – but this first Venetian occupation was shortlived, lasting for only seven years for in 1214 the island was annexed by the Despotate of Epiros, Michael II Dukas.

For reasons of expediency, he gave his daughter Helena in marriage to Manfred, King of the Two Sicilies, and Helena took to the marriage the island of Corfu as part of her dowry. But instability reigned in Italy, Manfred quarrelled with the Pope who promptly pledged his allegiance to Charles of Anjou, supporting his contention for the throne in Naples. Manfred was killed at the battle of Benevento and in 1267 Corfu was surrendered to the new King. Rulership of the island by the House of Anjou then lasted until 1386. Owing his throne to the Pope, Charles of Anjou forcibly imposed Catholicism upon the island: a Roman Catholic archbishop was installed and the biggest Orthodox churches were taken over. Like its Angevin rulers, Corfu experienced turbulent times until, in the final part of those days, it was left to its own devices and found itself with no option but to give itself up, once again, to the Venetians who had kept their eyes on the place ever since they were forced out in 1214. This time, they legalised their position and in 1402 bought the island from the Kingdom of Naples for 30,000 gold ducats. They ruled for four centuries, leaving indelible marks on the way of life here. They derived large revenues from the island – in taxes, by renting out lands, by trade. They encouraged the cultivation of the olive by offering twelve gold pieces for every hundred trees planted – an incentive that led to olives becoming the principal crop at the expense of others: so trade boomed, and the harbour was always busy. The Serene Republic strengthened the town's position by building a New Fort not far from the Old, and this still overlooks the town. In 1576 after successfully holding off a Turkish invading force the New and the Old Forts were linked by a wall on the western side, and the resultant fortification was very significant.

Another Turkish attempt to capture the place was made in 1716, when a force of about 30,000 landed on the eastern shores of the island. Fortunately, an Austrian Marshall in the service of the Venetians had laid his defensive plans carefully and, with the aid of a timely storm, he and his eight thousand defenders succeeded in demoralising the Turkish forces who beat an ignominious retreat having lost about half their number.

Nevertheless, the wars with Turkey took their toll, and Venice began to loose her power and influence in the Adriatic. In 1797 she fell to the forces of Napoleon Bonaparte who had declared that he would '.. be an Attila to the Venetian State'. A French fleet was sent to take possession of the island, which then became a 'departement' of France. The French occupation was as unpopular as the Venetian one before it and when a Russo-Turkish Alliance, which had been been running an effective campaign against the French, exploited the rising tide of local discontent it successfully turned the population against the regime which was then forced to capitulate to the Russian fleet which arrived on the doorstep.

Under the Treaty of Constantinople of 1800, the Ionian Islands became an autonomous state owing allegiance to the Ottoman Empire, and then in 1807, under the Peace of Tilsit, they were ceded once again to the French and the second period of French occupation lasted until 1814. This time the French were more careful, and the occupation created a good impression on the locals. Special attention was given to improving agricultural production, and education was widely promoted. French influence from this era is evident in some of the architecture in the town. The so-called 'French Arcades' which face onto the Spainada, or Esplanade, were designed by a Frenchman called de Lessups who had them built in 1807. Officially they are called 'The Liston', a name derived from a Venetian term for a 'List of Nobles'.

From 1809 the British were making their presence felt in the Ionian Islands, and when Napoleon fell in 1814 a proposal for independence was put forward to the Congress of Vienna. The Treaty of Paris in the following year recognised the islands as a free and independent nation under the protection of Britain and a Lord High Commissioner, to be headquartered in Corfu, was appointed. The first man to hold the post was Thomas Maitland who was, at the time of his appointment, commander in chief of British Forces in the Mediterranean and Governor of Malta.

The Greek War of Independence began in 1821, and attracted a deal of support from the locals. The British stamped this out in short order and did the same with the Unification Movement which followed the establishment of the Greek state. Freedom of the press was finally granted in 1848, and the islanders were at last allowed to express their support for Union with Greece, and Corfu, along with the other Ionian islands, was finally ceded to Greece in 1864. The 'quid pro quo' was Greek acceptance of a British-backed candidate to the Greek Throne. In 1862 the Chamber of Deputies elected a Danish Prince to the throne as King George I of Greece and soon afterwards, on May 1st 1864, the islands were united amid huge jubilations and celebrations in both Corfu and Athens. Although the treaties stated that the island was to remain neutral, it was used as a base for allied forces in WWI, was bombed by the Italians in 1940, and was badly damaged and occupied by the Germans in 1943 when they destroyed many public buildings and churches

Today, as you'll see, Corfu is a delight and is one of the top holiday destinations in all of Greece offering the whole spectrum of entertainment and relaxation – from brash, noisy seaside resorts (Corfu Town is not one of those!) to traditional villages and glorious mountain walks.

The harbour is on the northern side of the promontory on which the town stands and the port itself is divided into old and new. The former is nearer the town and is today devoted to small boats and to the innumerable ferries that ply between the island, the mainland and other islands. The new port, further to the west has a long pier for cruiseships but if there is a run on the place at any particular point in time they anchor off, running tenders to the drop off point where there is a modern terminal building housing the usual array of amenities. This is some distance from the town, fifteen to twenty minutes walk, and a shuttle service is usually provided – better by far, because those twenty minutes can be hot (and thirsty)! The bus will wend its way past the walls of the New Fort where the winged lion symbol of Venice can be seen sculpted into the walls themselves, lasting reminders of their builders. Five minutes through the back streets brings you to the Spainada, the huge esplanade that is the focal point of the town. Your shuttle will drop you off on the eastern edge of this, close to the waterfront and the massive walls of the Old Fort. Stand with this behind you and look across the Spainada for a few moments of orientation.

Directly ahead on the far perimeter is a row of large trees with dozens of open air restaurants nestling in their shade. Behind the trees stand the French Arcades, the main part of the town lying behind them. To your right, at three o'clock, the imposing façade of The Palace of St. Michael & St. George built during the early stages of British rule as a home for the Lord High Commissioner. Today the Palace houses the Museum of Asiatic Art, which I'll tell you more about a little later. The Palace is fronted by a bronze statue of Sir Frederick Adam, one of the British Lord High Commissioners. In the middle distance at the centre of the square is the only cricket pitch in Greece, and if you're here at the right time you'll see the locals at play! The road leading across the square is a popular parking area and taxi rank. A good way to see Corfu Town is by horse and carriage and they have a rank here as well. (Ask the fare!) Half way across the square and on this road you'll find an ancient Venetian wellhead which is worth having a look at.

To your left and at the lower end of the esplanade you'll find the Maitland Rotunda, built in the Ionic style and erected in honour of Sir Thomas Maitland. Behind you towers the Old Fortress, reached by a bridge over the Contafossa Moat. The fortress walls are enormous and encircle what was once the whole town. You can climb to the top of the ancient citadel, the Paleo Frourio, and be rewarded with fantastic views out to sea to the east and across the Spainada and the town to the west. On the south side of the Old Fort area you'll see the Church of St. George, built by the British in 1840 but modelled on a Doric Temple, its architecture contrasting sharply with that of the rest of the citadel.

Orientation over, it's time to explore.
Heading northwards and keeping the moat and Old Fort to your right, you'll pass beside a small fenced off park and come upon a pretty little Orthodox church called Panoyia Mandrakina. There are lovely views of one of the yacht marinas from the adjacent parapet. Move on into the heavily treed area to the right of the Palace and you'll come across a café and art gallery, then you're at the Palace itself, its imposing verandah frontage looking out over the head of Sir Frederick Adam to the cricket pitch on Spainada. The Palace houses the Museum of Asiatic Art whose major exhibit is a collection of some 10,000 items collected by a local diplomat during his travels overseas between 1850 and 1929. Pieces on show include statues, armour, items of silk and all sorts of ceramics from China, India, Japan and other Asiatic countries.

Leaving the Palace at its western side you'll be on a square called Platia Kole, home to more pavement cafes. Walk south from this and you'll be in Eleftherias Street, with the French Arcades on your right and those tree-shaded restaurants on your left with the Spainada behind. This area is always full of people and the cafes start filling up from about eleven thirty. Everything is colour and movement and this is a delightful place to pause awhile to watch the world go by and to reflect on the delights that you've seen so far. Rested, walk on past the French Arcades to an area of hotels. You'll find an Internet Café here, on the right, and a little further along the Archaeological Museum which is worth visiting for it is home to a Gorgon Frieze dating from the 6th century BC which originally formed part of the Temple of Artemis that I'll tell you more about once I take you out of the town itself. At the end of the street the Ionian Academy stands proud, the winged lion of Venice gracing its portal and gazing out over Garitza Bay, a wide sweep of water that lies between the promontory of the Old Fort and the next headland down the coast. Lined with hotels, there is a good beach and another marina here, and a number of waterfront cafes, their patrons sipping whatever they're sipping while enjoying the view, which is a delight.

You've now covered this area so walk back through the Spainada past the Maitland Rotunda and the rather imposing Bandstand: your goal now is the French Arcades and the town which lies behind them. Running parallel with Eleftherias to the rear of the Arcades is a road called Kapodistriou, and running at right angles off this and into the town proper are several streets. Take Agiou Spyridonos, one of the widest and one that is lined with shops selling just about everything – souvenirs, leathergoods, olive-wood, gold jewellery, ouzo – and the loquat liqueur that looks even better than it tastes!

Half way down its length on the left you'll reach Agios Spyridon, the church that is named after the island's patron saint, with its distinctive red domed belltower. The holiest place on the island, the church is home to a silver casket containing the mummified body of Spyridon who rose to become a bishop in his lifetime. He is said to have performed many miracles both before and after his death in AD350 and four times each year his casket is carried aloft through the streets. Outside the doors to the church is a shrine, where the faithful lodge lighted candles in supplication.

Turn left at the end of the street and you'll find the Paper Money Museum on your left and then a square called Plateia Dimarcheiou. This is Town Hall Square and is named after the elegant Venetian building which began life in 1663 as a meeting place for the city's elders and nobility. It became a theatre in 1720 and then the Town Hall in 1903 when the British added a second storey. The square is an attractive one, overlooked not only by the

Town Hall, but also by the Roman Catholic Cathedral of Agios Iakovos (also known as San Giacomo) and an imposing branch of the Bank of Greece. There are a couple of open-air restaurants in the square offering an inviting setting in which to enjoy a spot of refreshment.

Had you turned right instead of left at the end of Agiou Spryidon, in a block or two you would have reached the Mitropoli, the Greek Orthodox Church of the Madonna of the Cave – Panagia Spilitotissa. This became Corfu's orthodox cathedral in 1841 and is dedicated to a Byzantine Empress whose body lies in a silver coffin near the altar.

Walk northwards from the Mitropoli towards the waterfront which is bounded at this point by a road called Arseniou. From here there are panoramic views over the harbour and across the channel to the pine clad island lying enticingly off the northern shore. Again, there are lots of places along this stretch of seafront where you can pause awhile and have a drink and the beach below the parapet is popular with the locals, cooling off in the noonday sun.

The Byzantine Museum stands a few yards inland from Aresnoiu and is well worth a visit for it houses an impressive collection of 15th century icons and other artworks from the Cretan school. The museum occupies a renovated church, a wholly appropriate home for the mainly religious artefacts on display

Everything that I've talked about so far lies within easy walking distance of the Spainada except perhaps for the New Fort which is not, at any event, open to the public, being as it is a Greek Naval Base.

Corfu town is a delight – vibrant, colourful and hot by day, romantic and appealing by night when its pavement cafes glow beneath the trees, their menus full of temptation – Kavouras (broiled crab), Kalamares (barbecued squid), Astakos (lobsters served with olive oil) and Psaroupa (mussel and shellfish soup) as well as those classic and well loved Greek dishes, known to us all – Kleftiko, Souvlakia, Mousaka and Taramosalta. Delicious. I can recall one particularly happy evening ashore here in the hours before a midnight departure. Rosie and I dined in style with the ship's classical pianist – Nigel, if you're reading this, all I can say is 'thanks for the memory' – your beautifully rendered concertos were even more delightful ever afterward!

There will be an array of tours on offer. One of the most pleasing will take you to see the islet of Pondikonissi, Mouse Island, which lies just off Kanoni, a short bus ride to the south of Corfu town. Here the Church of the Pantokrator nestles amidst lush trees on the tiny island which is said to be the petrified ship of Odysseus (or one of them, at least!). Pondikonissi is featured so often in travel brochures that it has become almost a symbol of Corfu. Close by is another islet, joined to the land by a causeway and home to a little church and the Convent of Valcheron.

At the southern end of Galitsa Bay is the site of the ancient city of Kerkyra. Heading towards this from Corfu Town, you'll see the Tomb of Menekrates which was only discovered in 1843 during road construction work. A round structure of stone, it dates back to about 600 BC and archaeologists have determined that the inscription that it bears tells of a man called Menekrates who was consul of Kerkyra. Next you'll see the 11th century church of Saints Jason and Sosipater (Agion Iasonos kai Sosipatrou), those men who are said to have brought Christianity to the island. This is perhaps the most typical monument to the Byzantine period to be found anywhere on Corfu. Other archaeological remains nearby include The Temple of Artemis and, a little further south, the Temple of Kardaki. The Villa of Mon Repos, built in 1824 by Sir Frederick Adam as a gift for his wife and later gifted to the Greek Royal family is a popular attraction.

You may opt for a tour venturing further afield – perhaps to the slopes of Mount Pantokrator, 'The Almighty', which dominates the northeast bulge of the island, its peak rising to a height of 3,000 feet above the sea. A little road runs all the way to the top and this is a popular place for naturalists and walkers – although a hike to the top should not be approached lightly, as it is a very long way up. Nevertheless, whether you get to the top on foot, or by vehicle, you'll be well rewarded for the views of nearby Albania are stunning and in clear weather you can even see the coast of Italy, hazy on the western horizon.

There are many resorts strung out around the northern parts of the island – some with names familiar, maybe, from other holidays in a different time – Kassiopi, Sidari, Palaiokastritsa and Kalami. Each has its own appeal, nearly all offer typical tavernas on the beachfront, all enjoy views across a beautiful, sunlit sea.

Unless you're staying overnight, or have a late departure scheduled, you'll rejoin your ship as the heat of the day starts to fade. Slipping her moorings, her whistle sounding the customary goodbyes you'll glide out of the harbour with the lights of Corfu town winking on, the great, darkening bulk of the Old Fort looming to starboard and you're on your way northwards heading deeper into the Adriatic.

DUBROVNIK
Croatia

Sponza PalaceSponza

St. Blaise's Church

*Dubrovnik
The Old City*

Pile Gate

Old Harbour

Stradun

Onofrio's Well

Pile Gate

DUBROVNIK
Pearl of the Adriatic

Often described as the "Pearl of the Adriatic", Dubrovnik is situated on the eastern shores of the Adriatic, about half way between Corfu in the south and Venice in the north. Strategically located and protected by islands, Dubrovnik's development has always been based on maritime and merchant activities. Archaeological excavations show that there has been a settlement here since the 6th century or before, although its real prosperity took off with the intensified east/west traffic heralded by the Crusades of the 12th and 13th centuries.

Venice, the most powerful city state of the era, lies not far distant, and was the controlling influence here for a long time until Dubrovnik succeeded in securing liberation from the clutches of the Venetian doges by way of the Zadar Treaty of 1358.

The city fathers of the day successfully organised transit trade with the Balkan hinterland and then, under pressure from aggressive Turkish expansionism, accepted Turkish patronage in 1525: the 'quid pro quo' was a licence to trade, on preferential terms, with the whole Turkish Empire. Growing in importance, by the end of the 16th century Dubrovnik had formed itself into a Republic, with its own government, currency and flag and, as I've said, owed much to its maritime trade. During the 16th century the merchant fleet of which it was so proud and to which it owed so much numbered more than two hundred vessels and the city's maritime museum tells its story very well, with a wealth of artefacts that has kept this writer amused for many a long hour. But more about this museum later.

Trading does tends to run in cycles, and the highs of the 16th century gave way to lows of the 17th when a cyclical downturn was compounded by a catastrophic earthquake which hit the city in 1667. It took time to recover, and there were signs of economic recovery right up to Napoleon's arrival in 1808, when the Dubrovnik Republic finally succumbed. At the Congress of Vienna of 1815 the region became part of Croatia.

In our day, recent history tells of Serbia's aggression in this part of the world: in October 1991 Dubrovnik was fiercely attacked by the Serbs and Montenegrans, whose stated aim was to destroy it. The region was occupied and largely devastated, and the city itself was besieged for something like eight months, suffering continuous bombardment and truly barbarous damage. You may remember the horrific scenes that appeared on our television screens, when hundreds were killed, two thirds of all city's roofs were breached, nine palaces were gutted and more than five hundred of the historic buildings were severely damaged .

Thankfully, that era has gone, and most of Dubrovnik has been restored under the co-ordination of UNESCO which has declared it a World Heritage Site. Sadly, whilst the bullet holes and bomb damage have been patched up and the buildings restored to their former glory, tourism, upon which eighty percent of the population depends, is taking a long time to come back. For example, in 1990, British tourists numbered six hundred thousand whereas in 2001, ten years after those horrible events, they reached just over forty thousand. So sad, for such is the beauty of this place that it inspired George Bernard Shaw to say of it "Those who wish to see heaven on Earth should come to Dubrovnik".

If you, my readers, have not been here yet, you have a real treat in store for it is a city full of beautiful Gothic, Renaissance and Baroque churches, monasteries, palaces and fountains and you are going to fall in love with it, like so many who have come before you.

Dubrovnik's coastline is dotted with islands and it's really quite a small place with a resident population of something like sixty thousand who enjoy a pleasant climate of hot, dry, summers and mild, damp winters.
The hillsides are rich in a wide variety of fauna with cypress, pine and olive groves in abundance and a profusion of citrus fruits, aromatic herbs, flowers and vines.

An aerial view of the old city gives a good perspective and you can see the astonishing city walls, by far the most outstanding feature. The old city occupies the western part of a bay. Offshore to the south and east lies Lokrum Island, about which more later, whilst a promontory to the west is the site of the suburb called Lapad, home to a number of hotels and one or two holiday developments. At the northern side of Lapad in a wide inlet is the modern commercial port of Gruz, dominated at its western end by a magnificent, recently completed, suspension bridge.

Often cruiseships berth in Gruz, although sometimes they anchor off the Old City, between its ancient harbour and Lokrum island. In many visits to Dubrovnik I have only ever anchored once, so for the sake of this discussion, I'll assume your ship has followed the usual pattern and has tied up alongside. (If you are so fortunate as to anchor instead, then please disregard all that I'm about to say about the shuttle bus ride into the Old City – your tender journey is but a five/six minute boat ride, simpler by half. And the tender quay is a few yards from St. Blaise's Square, discussed in the paragraphs that follow).

The entrance to Gruz harbour is an attractive one and worth being up on deck to see. Rounding the Lapad peninsular, your ship will thread its way between beautiful little wooded islands, making for the harbour entrance.

The sail-in will give you a very good preview of the joys in store although you won't see anything of the Old City at this time – that treat is for later.

You are likely to tie up in the shadow of the suspension bridge that now dominates the Gruz harbour shoreline. Here you are about two miles from the Old City and a shuttle bus will almost certainly be provided: this will take you along the Gruz waterfront which is part cruiseship berths, part ferry terminal, part marina, but all attractive: then, past a bustling market, you're into the suburb of Gruz itself which is a modern, tree-lined place of large hotels and blocks of offices and flats. Heading eastward and up over the prow of a hill, you'll drop down on the other side to be suddenly confronted with the enormous walls of the Old City which appear, as if by magic, ahead of you and to your right. In a moment you're dwarfed beneath them until you emerge from their shadow into the coach park which stands outside the western gate which is called Pile (Pil-eh). This is the drop-off point (and, when you've finished and are ready to return, the pick-up one as well).

The shady square on the southern side of the bus stop has a parapet overlooking the sea and the towering walls form its eastern perimeter. A one-time drawbridge leads you across a dry moat to the Pile Gates themselves. You'll find local womenfolk on the bridge selling their crafts – mainly lacework – and as you enter the walls a minstrel dressed in national costume will be strumming a welcome on his guitar, its melody haunting. Then you're through the gates and the vista of the ancient buildings lining Placa Stradun, the main street, lies enticingly before you. This stretches the length of the city, in one straight line from the west, Pile Gate, to Luza Square in the east, and Luza Square is separated from the waterfront of the Old Harbour by just one building.

On your right stands the circular, domed bulk of Onofrio's Well (sometimes referred to as the Large Onofrio Fountain) which dates from about 1440 and is named after its builder, Onofrio di Giordano della Cava. Its dome was added later, in 1520, and was erected in thanksgiving for deliverance from a devastating earthquake earlier in the same year. Opposite and on your left is the Franciscan Monastery, the belltower of its church taller even than the mighty walls which are, I would guess, thirty of forty feet high at this point. You can go into the Monastery and the adjacent Church of Saint Saviour which was built on the order of the city's Senate in 1520. The Monastery houses an ancient pharmacy (said to date from 1317) which still functions as such – modern packets of aspirin alongside ancient phials and jars. In the Monastery, too, will be found the city's best collection of ancient manuscripts, a veritable Mecca for anyone wishing to study the literary labours of old Ragusans. In the library is a beautiful Reading Room where Sebastian Slade, preacher and historian, did much of his work: here his portrait hangs proudly as a reminder of his efforts.

A short distance down Placa and on your right is a Bureaux de Change and a Tourist Information point where the staff is helpful and informative. All manner of guidebooks and books about the city are on sale here, many of them graphically depicting the woes of 1991. The local currency is the Croatian Kuna (about eleven to the pound, last time I was here). You'll need a few for wholly 'local' purchases – buying a ticket to go up onto the walls, for instance – but don't change more than the minimum for your requirements – it is a 'non-negotiable' currency and you won't be able to change it back into sterling, certainly not at home, anyway.

All the way along the length of Placa you'll find art galleries, boutiques, bookshops and souvenir outlets – there is no shortage of things to buy nowadays, all the locals want are the people to buy them! Someone hereabouts makes the most intricate and detailed model sailing ships which are expensive but very beautiful: cheaper ones, fine as souvenirs but not wonderful models, can also be had as reminders of Dubrovnik's maritime past.

At the eastern end of Placa you'll find yourself in Luza Square with St. Blaise's Church on its right hand side, a statue of the saint himself gazing proudly down from his gable perch, watching in silence the milling hordes below. The church, a fine Baroque building, is open to the public and is dark and cool inside. Another statue of the saint, this time a bronze, stands next to the altar. St. Blaise is said to have saved the city from a Venetian attack in the 10th century. Orlando's column stands in the centre of the square. This was erected in 1428 and was the point from which all the city's decrees were proclaimed.

Onofrio's Fountain (or the 'Little Onofrio Fountain as it is sometimes called) is on the wall of the building on the eastern side of the square, whilst on the northern side stands the Sponza Palace. Built in 1520, the Palace has an elegant Gothic façade, is one of the oldest of Dubrovnik's medieval buildings and today functions as the City Hall. In one of its ground floor rooms, open to the public, is a rather sad display of photographs of Dubrovnik under siege and a gallery of pictures of those who lost their lives at hands of the aggressor a short decade or so ago.

Do an about turn now, and you'll have Sponza Palace behind you and St. Blaise's Church on your right. At the head of the street into which you are now heading stands the Cathedral, a small but glorious old place whose original construction is said to have been funded by our own King Richard the Lionheart, who found shelter here in 1192 after being shipwrecked on his voyage home from a Crusade.

The building that he paid for was wrecked by the earthquake of 1667 but the locals are a resilient lot and they began work on a new church which took five hundred years to build and stands today in fine Gothic style, awaiting your visit. The Cathedral Treasury displays a number of quite exceptional exhibits including St. Blaise's skull wearing a Byzantine crown.

Just before you reach the cathedral on your left hand is the Rector's Palace, said by many to be the city's finest building. This too suffered earthquake damage and has been extensively restored. Our old friend Onofrio designed it, and building work was started in 1435. It was the headquarters for the city's council as well as the home of the ruling Rector, a man who held office for only one month at a time to avoid any possibility of being tempted into corruption. Inside you can visit the Rector's rooms, the former State Offices and the Dubrovnik Museum, with its collection of coins, medals, seals, weapons and the like.

Behind the cathedral is Gundulic Square, the site of a bustling open-air market. This is always thronged with people, visitors and locals alike, and if you're after a true flavour of the city, this is the place for you. Fruit sellers, lace makers, vegetable stalls, lavender vendors, all vying for your business. I have gazed in fascination at the arrays of the local plonk and on one memorable occasion succumbed to the insistence of a zealous stall holder who persuaded me to part with some money – about 75p, as I recall – and I left, clutching the litre bottle protectively under my arm, impatient to get back to the ship to sample the delights of its clear, almost oily, contents.

To cut a long story short, on arrival in my cabin I poured a generous tot, topped it up with ice cold coke and took a long, thirsty, mouthful. Retrieving my head (or so it seemed) from the deck, I gazed at the still-nearly-full-bottle in awe, and wondered what I should do with it. It so happened that on that particular cruise I had befriended the ship's Bosun (the man on board who is responsible for the upkeep of the decks), and I gave it to him. He gratefully accepted – then avoided me for a day or two until the third day (by which time Dubrovnik was but a pleasant memory), when I cornered him on deck and asked him how he had enjoyed it. 'The best paint stripper I've ever had', he muttered, failing to look me in the eye. So, you have been warned!

The stall holders are ever ready to let you taste, try, examine – in the hopes that you will buy, of course. It did occur to me how unlike our own markets this place is – or at least, the market in my town, where the stall holders are not a friendly lot.

The market square is surrounded by open air cafes and the wines and seafoods (particularly the grilled calamari) is divine, and quite inexpensive.

Head south and west from the market and you'll find yourself at the foot of the Jesuit steps, at the head of which stands the Church of St. Ignatius, named after Ignatius Loyola, the man who founded the Jesuit order. Commonly dubbed the Jesuit Church this fine Baroque structure was built to the design of Andrea Pozzo at the end of the 17th century. Paintings inside include works by Gaetano Garcia, who decorated the apse with scenes from the life of the saint.

Retrace your steps down the Jesuit steps, turn left at their foot and in a few blocks you'll come upon the Rupe Museum a fascinating place where, back in the 15th century, fifteen enormous underground silos were carved out of the solid rock as a hedge against siege.

Two blocks to the north of the Rupe you're back in the Placa almost opposite the Franciscan Monastery – and this is as good a time as any to venture up on those walls. Alongside St. Saviour's Chruch a staircase takes you to the top, almost directly above the Pile Gate. Here you'll need some local currency, for half way up is a ticket office which does not take foreign currency and a visit to the top of the walls will cost you a few Kuna. Reach the top and look down over the length of Placa: Onofrio's Well will be to your right, the Franciscan Monastery to your left, its campanile immediately in front. At the far end stands the town clocktower adjacent to St. Blaise's Church, and the vista of ancient ochre roofs stretches in every direction. It is absolutely wonderful – and the pause will give you a chance to catch your breath before pressing on with your expedition! To your left is the highest part of the wall with the Minceta Fortress at the apex. Climb to that, and be rewarded with the finest views of all – but do note that the climb is quite steep and can be a little slippery underfoot if it's been raining. From Minceta the wall gradually descends toward the Old Harbour and another of the defensive fortresses, Fort Revelin: next to this is the Domincan Monastery and as your wall ticket allows for multiple access you might like to visit this, since you're now at its doorstep.

Work on the building was started in 1228, but the complex only reached its present size in the 15th century. The monastery itself is pleasant enough with cool and serene cloisters, but it is the Museum which occupies part of the building that is of particular interest, especially for the art lovers amongst you who want to pore over the works, mainly religious, which date from the 15th and 16th centuries. Several manuscripts, sculptures and religious artefacts are to be seen, and the museum and adjacent library are certainly worth a browse. Many of Dubrovnik's nobles are buried in the Monastery grounds.

Back on the walls their lowest point is on the landward side of the old harbour before they climb once more to St. John's Fortress, the bastion on its southern entrance. This houses the Maritime Museum that I mentioned at the beginning of this chapter, and lovers of ships and the sea as well as those wanting to know more about the city's maritime past should not miss it. Spread over a couple of floors it comprehensively covers most ages, with some excellent ship models, nautical instruments, charts and manuscripts, uniforms, photographs and marine weaponry of all kinds on display. There are spectacular views out over the bay from the roof of the museum, with the coastline stretching away to the tiny resort of Cavtat, clearly visible on the most distant headland. Lokrum Island is about a mile offshore at this point, its wooded shoreline beckoning – more about this in a few moments.

You can complete your stroll around the walls on the seaward side (they are relatively flat now, affording views over all the town's sights with which you are now familiar) and then you'll find yourself back where you started, above the Pile Gate. If you've walked the full circuit of the walls you've covered about a mile and a half along ramparts which were started in the 10th century! Wonderful.

A few practical tips, before we venture a little further afield.

Remember my advice about the currency – don't change too many of your own hard earned bucks for Kuna, as you'll find it difficult to change back. But you will need some Kuna for minor incidentals.
The marble-paved Placa can be slippery when wet.
The streets to the north side of Placa are quite steep, whereas those on its southern side are easier going.
Many organised excursions actually finish at the Old City rather than back at the port – a good idea, because it ensures that everyone has the opportunity to visit this beautiful place as well as taking a tour – but this does mean that the queues for the returning shuttle busses can be quite long, so get to the bus stop in good time.

Now, much is said these days about the Croatian Riviera, and in Dubrovnik you are at its heart. But you may have been here before and want to see further afield so let's look at some things to see away from the city.

Your ship will assuredly be offering a tour to Cavtat, a picturesque seaside resort that grew from the ruins of Roman Epidaurus, destroyed in the 7th century by invading Avar tribes. Cavtat lies about half an hour's coach ride to the south of Dubrovnik, and the coach journey is pleasing. Leaving the quayside, your coach will climb to the heights up above the Old City where you'll probably stop for a photo-shoot, as the view of the city from here is unparalleled. Your coach will head inland for a short time through the countryside of Zupa Dubrovacka (Parish of Dubrovnik) before winding its

way back to the coast at Cavtat which has a pleasing, palm lined promenade and a town centre that is a pleasant place to wander through with its
profusion of cafes, restaurants and souvenir shops. Atop the hill overlooking the town sits the impressive, domed, octagonal building that is the
Racic Mausoleum. The work of a Croatian sculptor called Ivan Mestrovic,
the building commemorates the death of a family wiped out by plague:
climb the 125 steps up to the mausoleum and be rewarded with the views
from the top – be sure you've timed it right, as you'll need to get back to
your coach in time for its departure or you'll find yourself spending rather
more time in Croatia than you bargained for. If you're feeling less energetic
and can't face those 125 steps, sit by the waterfront and watch your fellow
passengers making the climb – they'll be sure to tell you about it!

If you're determined to be independent during your visit to Dubrovnik you
can actually get to Cavtat on your own – take a taxi (it is only twelve or so
miles away) or catch a boat from Dubrovnik's Old Harbour. These run
regularly, and there are kiosks on the harbour waterfront which advertise
prices and departure times. Once again, remember to make sure you've
got your timings right!

From the same spot on the waterfront you can catch a boat to nearby Lokrum Island. Your ship may be offering a tour which embraces this and one
or two of the other islands, and if it does, then do consider it because the
islands are beautiful. But Lokrum is very easy to reach on your own for the
boats run very regularly, the trip is only about twenty minutes and offers
the added benefit of lovely views of the Old City, this time from the water.
Lokrum is a nature reserve and very popular with tourists and residents
alike, who flock here over week-ends: part of its eastern shoreline is a popular naturist beach.

It is an historic place: in the 12th century a group of Benedictine monks
built a monastery here and you can stroll through its gardens and sense
the peace that must have motivated the monks all those years ago (the
naturist beach was not here, in those days). At the landing stage is a useful map which points the way to the monastery, its gardens, and the clutch
of open air cafes and restaurants that nestle in strategic spots beneath the
trees, the views offered from some of their parapets are breathtaking.

If a multi-island tour is on offer, you'll probably visit Kolocep, famed for its
corals and Lopud, home to many of those trailblazing sailors who made
their perilous voyages taking the produce of their country to the four corners of their world.

Whatever you do during your visit, I can guarantee that you'll leave much
happier for having seen Dubrovnik and I'm sure that you'll concur absolutely with George Bernard Shaw's accolade, worth repeating, "If you want
to visit heaven on earth, come to Dubrovnik".

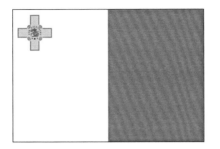

VALLETTA
Malta

Malta, GC

The Law Courts

The co-cathedral of St. John

Grand Harbour view

Valletta skyline

The co-cathedral of St. Paul, Mdina

VALLETTA
Malta, GC

Our next destination, Malta, has a very long history indeed – and a fascinating one. The earliest chapters are lost in the distant past, but the oldest traces of human occupation go back to about the fifth millennium BC. In clear weather the islands can be seen from Cape Passero on the southern tip of Sicily, and the sixty odd mile crossing from there would not have presented any real problems to the adventurers of that day, who could easily have coveted some virgin lands upon which to set up a new home. Perhaps they were those earliest inhabitants?

But it was the Phoenicians, said to have arrived here about eight hundred years before Christ, who gave the island its name – and they called it Maleth (or Malet), which meant Shelter, or Haven. It's interesting that Homer's name for Calypso's Island, "Neesos Kalupsous" translates into English as "The Island of the Hiding Place" – clearly, Homer had heard of this haven, somewhere in the remote sea, and concluded that it was a fitting home for his Calypso, the Goddess of the Cave. Today, high above a sandy beach in Ramla Bay on the north coast of Gozo, you'll still find Calypso's Cave, and the spot where the goddess bewitched Odysseus on his way from the Trojan War. All quite exciting stuff, I'm sure you'll agree!

More or less in the dead centre of the Mediterranean and blessed with the finest harbour in the whole of this ocean, there is little wonder that successive populations wanted to keep the islands for themselves – and they fortified them, guarded them, and went to extraordinary lengths to protect them, as we shall see. From offshore, they must look today rather as they did in bygone times – impregnable and forbidding

In the course of the 6th century BC the islands passed to the Carthaginians who were, at the time, in the process of consolidating their power in Sicily – part of a grand plan to build a trading empire in the Western Mediterranean. The islands remained a part of the Punic Empire for the next three hundred years until, in 257BC, they were invaded and seriously plundered by the Roman Army. Possession then see-sawed for a period until in 218BC, the start of the second Punic War, when Rome finally took possession under a man called Sempronius who incorporated the islands into the Roman province of Sicily.

In both Punic and Roman times the principal town was on the site of present day Mdina, the importance of which at that time is evident from the considerable number of tombs and catacombs found in neighbouring Rabat. There is much evidence, too, to support the view that the islands enjoyed prosperity during the early Roman period, when they achieved fame as the producers of fine cloth.

Probably the most famous event in Malta's history during its domination by Rome relates to Christ's apostle Paul: on his way to imprisonment in Rome, he was shipwrecked here in about AD60 and you can read the Biblical account in the Book of Acts where Chapter 28 Verse 1 reads *"....when we had made it to land we learned that the island was called Malta"*.
St. Paul's Bay lies on the north coast of the island and is supposedly where the apostle landed on that fateful night.

Apart from the exploits of Paul the history books are otherwise rather vague for a long period with the islands disappearing from view until 533AD when Belisarius, General to Byzantine Emperor Justinian, called here on his way to sort out the Vandals in North Africa. At a time when life was anything but a bed of roses and the future looked bleak indeed, I encountered the story of the Byzantine General, who had a noteworthy philosophy – *"God ever loves to help those who help themselves, but God help those who do not"*. Shortly after learning this quite useless snippet of information I encountered a rather ragged and forlorn looking teddy bear in the shop of an equally forlorn cross channel ferry and I bought him, because I felt that the motto fitted his demeanour – and he was named Belisarius in a short but touching ceremony just outside the breakwater of Dieppe harbour. He has sailed with me ever since and has spent many a long hour listening to me spout about the delights of the next port of call.

Back to Malta. In 870AD came the conquering Aghlabid Caliphs – Arabs who were by this time already masters of much of Spain and the southern shores of France, Italy and Sicily. They changed the name to Malta and introduced cotton and citrus fruit to the islands, remaining here until ousted by Count Roger of Normandy in 1090. Once more possession of the islands changed hands quite frequently, passing between Norman, Hohenstaufen, Aragonese and Barbary rulers until 1530 when Emperor Charles V made over Malta and its dependencies, in perpetual sovereignty, to the Order of St. John of Jerusalem. The Knights of St.John belonged to a nursing Brotherhood which originated in a small chapel and hospital set up in the first half of the 11th century in Jerusalem to provide succour to the sick and poor pilgrims to the Holy Sepulchre. They didn't remain a simple nursing brotherhood for long, and were soon spreading terror and dismay among Saracen armies everywhere. They shared in the Christian defeat at Tiberias, when Jerusalem was finally lost to Saladin. Then, from a new base on Rhodes they defied the Turks for two centuries until 1522 when Suleyman laid siege to their citadel and eventually drove them off the island, first to Crete and then to Malta, where their galleys soon began to prey on Muslim shipping. But, you can be sure that Islam didn't allow them to get away with it for long and in 1565 one hundred and eighty one ships carrying thirty thousand troops sailed from Constantinople's Golden Horn, bound for Malta – defended by the Knights and about eight thousand men. The Turkish landing was virtually unopposed in Marsaxlokk Bay, to which I'll take you a little later in our story. The Maltese were steadfast in the defence of their island, held out for a long hot summer in what was to become known as the Great Siege, and eventually drove the Turks away. The town of Valletta was born as of that time, named after Jean de Vallette, the Grand Master of the day.

In time the Knights lost their appetite for military adventures and turned their attention to trade, consolidating the advantages of their islands' unique geographic position and capitalising on its wonderful Grand Harbour, where your ship is just about to berth.

Not only were the islands in an enviable position from the point of view of trade – they were also hugely valuable from a strategic viewpoint, and were the object of many a covetous gaze in the various chancelleries of Europe. In June 1798 Napoleon, convoying a huge detachment of troops to Egypt, stopped here and demanded water for his ships but was refused, so he fiercely attacked, met with little resistance, captured Valetta and promptly evicted the Knights. Within three days the Order departed never to return, whereupon the French looted everything in sight, despoiled many churches, introduced draconian anti-clerical measures and made themselves extremely unpopular in the process. The Battle of the Nile and Nelson's victory led to Malta's plea for British help and Nelson set up a blockade under Captain Alexander Bell, who successfully starved the French into surrender and established *de facto* British rule on the island, a position that was confirmed by the Treaty of Paris of 1814: it wasn't long before Malta became an important Mediterranean base for the Royal Navy, vitally situated as it is for the effective acquisition of more colonies in the East and essential to the prosecution of the Crimean War and those conflicts that were to follow.

Various attempts were made to establish forms of self-government but these were largely unsuccessful for a variety of reasons. Malta was once again under siege for three weeks in June 1940, and stories abound of the heroics displayed during those dark and difficult days. She was a central plank in Wavell's advance on Tripoli and her aircraft and submarines severly complicated things for Rommel's adventures in North Africa. The year 1942 was crucial but the island survived and was awarded the George Cross, Britain's highest civilian decoration, in April 1942. The award is recorded for posterity on a plaque displayed on the wall of the Armoury which reads

"To the Governor, Malta: To Honour her brave people I award the George

Cross to the island fortress of Malta, to bear witness to a heroism and devotion that will long be famous in history. George, April 1942".

In 1947 the British Government gave £30 million towards reconstruction of the war-torn island, and for a time it was proposed that Malta be integrated into the United Kingdom. This plan foundered, and the island became independent in September 1964 with the Queen, at the islanders' request, remaining as monarch. A defence agreement gave British Forces the right to remain for ten years following independence and during this time Britain provided significant capital aid to help with economic development and diversification. More negotiations followed and a new agreement reached, which granted British and NATO forces the right to remain on the island until 1979, when they finally pulled out after one hundred and eighty years. Today, Malta is a Democratic Republic within the Commonwealth and the Office of Governor-General has, of course, been abolished in favour of the office of President.

Described as the finest in the Mediterranean, Valetta's Grand Harbour presents a magnificent vista to arriving cruiseships. Even if you've become accustomed to enjoying the warmth and comfort of your cabin until the sun is well up in the sky, do break the mould for your arrival here for you won't want to miss it.

Valletta occupies a heavily fortified promontory that juts into the sea on the north eastern shore of the main island. Fort St. Elmo at the seaward end of the city guards the harbour approaches, the city skyline dotted with spires, domes and turrets. The sweep of the harbour is bounded on the opposite, southern, shore by the towns of Vittoriosa, Cospicua and Seneglea, which are really sprawling suburbs although they like to retain their individual identities.

Cruiseships berth alongside the northern shore of Grand Harbour, at the foot of the hill upon which Valletta stands and from the berth it is a fifteen minute walk into the centre – not too far, but pretty steep. Taxis will be on the quayside, and a stall sells taxi tickets for specific journeys – a useful concept which ensures a measure of price uniformity and means you don't have to haggle with individual taxi drivers. You can also take a Karrozini, a horse and trap arrangement often referred to as the 'Maltese Cab' – do establish the fare to your destination first before climbing aboard!

For the sake of our discussion, let's assume you've decided to walk. Beyond the dock gates the road climbs quite steeply for a couple of hundred yards when it swings to the right almost at the base of a flight of steps which are the shortest route to the top. Seldom overcrowded (perhaps there's a message there) you won't be hassled during your climb and will have ample opportunities to pause and admire the harbour views from strategic points along the way. Reaching the top you'll find yourself in an area of gardens where a War Memorial does what War Memorials do.

One of the most noticeable things about Valletta, and indeed the whole of the island, is the lack of grass: but that is not to say that it devoid of vegetation – it's not, for there are trees and flowering shrubs a-plenty and it's pretty if not beautiful. At this point you'll be just beneath those enormous ramparts, absolutely splendid in their golden hue. This is an area of much activity and hustle and bustle, for it is the hub of Malta's bus system and the antiquity of the buses will not escape your notice! They are all painted in shades of red and orange and all seem to date from the 1950s or thereabouts: but despite their age and rattletrap appearance they certainly work, and residents and tourists alike use them to get about the city and the island cheaply and reliably. There is a constant buzz here with these colourful beasts streaming in and out from all points of the compass. A kiosk near at hand, nestling between stalls selling garish coloured drinks and sticky buns, provides bus information for the adventurous wanting to use the island's equivalent to Stagecoach.

The area just outside the City Walls which includes the bus terminus is dominated by the Triton Fountain, a rather grandiose affair designed by one Vincenzo Apap, and just nearby is a towering Monument to Christ the King and the Meridien Hotel.

Stand with your back to this and you'll be facing the main City Gates which stand on the other side of another of the town's principal defences – an enormous, dry moat commonly referred to as the ditch: about thirty feet wide and fifty feet deep this was hewn from solid rock by large numbers of unfortunate Turkish slaves way back in the city's chequered past. Cross over it by way of the bridge that leads to the City Gate and you'll get a clear understanding of just how seriously the Knights of St. John took the matter of defending their city.

The City Gate itself, tastelessly re-built in 1966, is not a beautiful structure but pass through it you must to arrive in Freedom Square, site of the old railway station before Malta's train service was discontinued and its lines removed in 1931. The left hand side of the square was arcaded in 1968, whilst the right is occupied by the ruins of the Royal Opera House, designed by E.M. Barry and built between 1861 and 1864 and demolished by bombs in 1942. Straight ahead is the thronged pedestrianised Republic Street, the central artery of Valetta which is closed to traffic except for shop deliveries which are supposed to happen only in the early afternoon. A short way along Republic you'll find the church of the Langue of Provence, St. Barbara. Sandwiched between buildings on either side, it is not readily identifiable as a church except that its rather austere façade is adorned with a gilded figure of the virgin which distinguishes it from its very commercial neighbours. The church was built in about 1739.

Next on the right, just off Republic Street in its own square stands the Co-Cathedral of St. John, built between 1573 and 1577 by Gerolamo Cassar. Until 1798 this was the conventual church of the Order of the Knights and all but two of the Grand Masters of the Order are buried here, their tombs comprising a veritable museum of Baroque sculpture. By Papal decree, the church was elevated to the status of Co-Cathedral in 1816, sharing the title with the Cathedral of Saints Peter and Paul in the old city of Mdina. The whole interior is colourful and filled with works of art – the ceiling by Treti, sculptures by Algardi, tapestries by Judocus de Vos and, above the altar, a masterpiece by Caravaggio "The beheading of St. John". Have a look, too, at the marble floor – really quite distinctive!

Returning to and continuing along Republic Street you'll reach Great Siege Square which is dominated by the colonnaded and imposing frontage of the Law Courts, then it's on into Republic Square with its flower kiosks and pleasant, shaded, pavement cafes where you can stop to slake your thirst on a glass of Maltese wine, or perhaps a local lager – both very drinkable! Here you'll find a marble statue of Queen Victoria standing in front of the National Library, which houses not only an impressive collection of some sixty thousand volumes but also the priceless archives of the Order.

The Grand Master's Palace is next on your right. Started in 1571, the front façade is nearly three hundred feet long and is pierced by two Baroque portals. This building remained the official residence of the Grand Master until Napoleon ousted him in 1798: over the years since it has been residence of the Governor General and latterly that of the President of the Republic of Malta and seat of the House of Representatives. Parts of the building are open to the public and the former Council Chamber of the Order, today known as the Tapestry Chamber, is adorned by a fine set of Gobelin Tapestries. In the adjacent Armoury Hall can be seen a fair collection of armour and weaponry from the period of the Knights. That plaque commemorating the award of the George Cross is affixed to the outside wall as is a chart which proudly displays all the coats of arms of all the successive Grand Masters who ruled here.

On the opposite side of Palace Square is a building known as the Guard Room where the inscription over the door records the cession of Malta to Great Britain. Palace Square itself is largely devoted to a car park and Karrozini (Maltese Cab) rank.

Continue northwards on your walk up Republic Street and in six blocks you'll reach Fort St. Elmo, inside of which is the National War Museum where re-enactments of various military events in the island's history are a regular feature.

Running parallel to Republic Street on its southern side is Merchants Street where you'll find the local market with its host of stalls selling all sorts of goodies. Keep on Merchants and you'll pass the Catholic Church of Our Lady of Damascus and the Municipal Palace before you arrive back at the Co-Cathedral of St. John. Next is is the Auberge de Castille, the office of the Prime Minister. Regarded as being the finest example of the architectural style known as Maltese Baroque, the auberge was designed and built by the architect Andrea Belli for Grand Master Pinto in 1741. The Upper Barracca Garden, notable for their splendid views are nearby and from here there is a splendid view across Grand Harbour.

Two streets paralleling Republic Street on its northern side are Strait Street and Old Bakery Street and I mention them because the old military men amongst you will want to know that the first used to be better known as 'The Gut', and the second is home to the Manoel Theatre, said to be one of the oldest theatres anywhere in Europe that is still in use. Here the Knights of old were entertained and you can take a guided tour through its gilded galleries and admire the richly decorated ceiling.

To round off your walk through this ancient place, stop by the Museum of Fine Arts in Vassali Street. This is another fine 18th century building that was the one time residence of the Royal Navy's Commander-in-Chief but today houses a fine collection of art including works by Tintoretto and Carpacio. Finally, back near Freedom Square, you can visit the Museum of Archaeology in the Auberge de Provence.

Before leaving the city to explore more of the island, a word about the fortifications. Designed by a man called Laparelli, they were built between 1566 and 1570 and are largely unaltered from those days. If you really want to get a better idea of their extent you can walk their length – it takes about an hour and a half to do so but the rewards are beautiful views across Grand Harbour and the cities of Vittoriosa, Cospicua and Senglea to the south, and Marsamextt Harbour and Sliema to the north.

On the landward side of the peninsular on which Valletta stands is Floriana, a sort of suburban extension of Valletta which is separated from Valletta proper by a set of rather magnificent gates called the Portes des Bombes built between 1697 and 1720.

Marsamextt Harbour is another extremely attractive inlet that attracts yachts by the hundred. Manoel Island at its centre is protected by another ancient fort at its seaward end and the smart suburb of Sliema nestles along its northern shore. Sliema beach is the nearest to your ship and is a twenty minute cab ride away. Some of you might like to play a round of golf, and will be pleased to know that temporary membership is available at the Marsa Sports Club which is but a short distance out of town and you shoppers will need to know that, since 2008, the currency here is the Euro. Good buys are honey, glassware, Maltese lace and cloth and, of course, Mdina glass for which the island is well known.

Let's venture out from Valletta and see some more of this famous island that has become a popular holiday destination in recent years.

Most ships will offer an excursion to the original capital Mdina, going on then to the nearby town of Mosta. Both are well worth visiting, so I'll start with Mdina, a mellow, serene old place dubbed the 'Silent City' for reasons which soon become obvious as you stroll its peaceful, narrow streets which are mostly pedestrianised. Entrance to the city is by way of a bridge and an elaborate, decorated archway, the city within dominated by the Cathedral of St. Peter & St. Paul, a dignified if rather austere building which stands on the spot where the apostle Paul during his enforced visit of AD60 is said to have converted Publius, Island Chieftan, to Christianity.

The Cathedral lays claim to having one of Europe's leading religious museums within its portals: inside it you'll see an icon said to have been painted by Christ's apostle Luke. The building itself is iconic, its floor covered with heraldic slabs commemorating various church dignitaries and its ceiling frescoed with scenes from the life of Paul, lovingly painted by Vincenzo and Antonio Manno.

The streets may be narrow, serene and reminiscent of a bygone age, but there is nothing ancient about the souvenir shops, and one of Malta's most famous exports is Mdina glass, not dissimilar from the Venetian variety but a little less expensive. Near the Cathedral is an outlet that specialises in this product, and they'll even parcel it up and ship it home for you if you're disinclined to take it away with you. Many tours to Mdina include lunch or tea which could well be served in a restaurant that commands superb views over the surrounding countryside from its parapets – for Mdina is built on top of a hill, the crest of which is about five hundred feet above sea level. Surrounding Mdina is Rabat, birthplace of Maltese Christianity and site of the catacombs mentioned earlier.

Not very far away is the town of Mosta, absolutely dominated by its massive Church of the Assumption of St. Mary. This was built between 1833 and 1860 and its dome ranks third in the world in size after St. Peter's in Rome and Hagia Sophia in Istanbul. The dome has another claim to fame:

in 1942 it was hit by three Axis bombs, one of which fell through into the crowded church below, rolled across the floor and failed to explode. Miraculously noone was hurt and the (now de-fused!) bomb is kept in the vestry as a memento of that frightening occasion. Your tour may take you on to the little village of Siggiewi which has a pleasant central square: if it does, it'll likely call next at Dingli Cliffs, from where you can look out on Filfa Island, longtime target for artillerymen practicing their art from below the cliffs on which you're standing.

Mdina, Mosta and Dingli are easily accessible if you want to be independent, as they all lie within a ten mile radius of Valletta.

One of the island's prettiest places is south east of Valletta – Marsaxlokk (pronounced Ma-sha-shloss), again less than ten miles from Valletta. Here is where the Turks landed at the start of the Great Siege of 1565. Today it is a very pretty fishing village, marred only by the chimneys of a nearby industrial complex. It's waterfront is a clutter of restaurants, souvenir stalls, cafes and fishing boats whose prows are colourfully adorned with massive painted 'eyes' necessary, the locals believe, to ward off the influences of evil spirits. This is an excellent place in which to pause awhile and try the local wine, which is excellent – in fact, one cruise line that I know of offers excursions to the wine cellars of a local vintner called Marsovin: if yours does so, then I can recommend it.

Other tours visit Vittoriosa on the southern shores of Grand Harbour. The Knights originally established themselves here when they first arrived on the Island and there is quite a lot to see including the Freedom Monument, the Parish Church of St. Lawrance and the Inquisitor's Palace, which was used as a Law Court intil 1574. One of its unusual features is the very low door which forced those entering to face their judges to bow in subservience. Beneath the Court you can still visit the dungeons where the condemned were incarcerated.

Next on the agenda is the Maritime Museum which occupies a building that used to be the old Royal Naval bakery. Here you'll find more fine models and paintings which tell the story of the island's maritime past. Finally, you may want a flutter at Malta's Casino de Venezia, located in what was the Captain's Palace whose commanding views across Grand Harbour may distract you from the losses that you may be incurring on the tables!

A popular tour is a boat ride around the waterways of Grand Harbour. On this one you'll see much of what I've been describing, but it always looks a little different from the water and the guide on the boat will give a running commentary as you cruise by Msida Creek and the Kalkara Boatyards – names that will bring back many memories to those of you who served here, perhaps during your days of National Service.

Finally, Malta does possess some remarkable archaeological sites at the Ghar Dalam Caves and the Hagar Qim Temples. Here you'll see the place thought to be the original home of the Neolithic settlers of some 6000 years ago and you'll wonder at the temples which testify to the island's great importance in the mists of a distant past. Maybe you'll ponder on the reasons why the island's temple-building civilisation suddenly disappeared 2500 years before Christ: if you hit on the answer do let me know for you'll be unique, because no-one else has come up with a plausible solution. But, thanks to painstaking excavations conducted in 1839 much can still be seen of that ancient civilisation.

I started this chapter by saying that you'll find your arrival in Grand Harbour absolutely spectacular: well, so is your departure. Invariably, your leaving will be in the late afternoon when the heat has gone out of the sun, and you'll glide between those magnificent, golden ramparts where many of the locals will be waving you away from the colonnades of the Lower Barracca Gardens, in the shadow of the historic Siege Bell Memorial.

Malta is a place that you will either love, or hate – and in my experience, you'll love it for it offers many things: antiquity and serenity alongside hustle and bustle, orange busses in profusion, wonderful artworks in its various churches and museums and a warmth amongst its people that is matched by its truly Mediterranean climate.

And one of the most magnificent harbours that you're likely to encounter, certainly in this sea.

You'll be back!

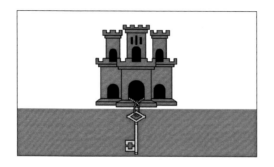

GIBRALTAR
Gibraltar

'The Convent'

Cathedral of the Holy Trinity

The 'Rock'

Barbary Ape

Old City Hall

View from Cablecar

Pillars of Hercules

'Duty Free!'

GIBRALTAR
Mighty Pillar of Hercules

Gibraltar is at the southernmost extremity of mainland Europe, and stands majestically at the entrance to the Mediterranean. It is connected to Spain by way of a mile long isthmus which is today the site of Gibraltar airport.

Known to the Phoenicians as Calpe, Gibraltar forms the northern Pillar of Hercules, the southern one being the mountain adjacent to Ceuta in Spanish Morocco, fifteen miles across the straits.

Invaded by the Moors in 711AD, the rock was originally named "Gib el Tarik", or Tarik's mountain, after the Moorish leader who led the conquest.

It's quite unique, because it is a town that is also a country which has been a British Crown Colony since 1711. It is almost universally known, affectionately, as "Gib" or "The Rock" and is blessed with a recorded history that goes back a little over twelve hundred years – although traces of cave dwellers, said to date back some forty thousand years, have been found. In 1848 an ancient female skull was discovered in Forbes Quarry, at the foot of the steep north face of the Rock, eight years before an identical skull was found in the Neander Valley, near Dusseldorf. So, in fact, Neanderthal Man, thought by many to be man's near ancestor, should really have been Gibraltarian Woman!

The two and a quarter square mile area has been, successively, in the hands of the Phoenicians, the Moors and the Spanish until the British established sovereignty by the Treaty of Utrecht which concluded the Spanish War of Succession. Ever since, Gibraltar has been a bone of contention between Spain and Great Britain, a dispute that reached its height in 1966 when Franco closed off the narrow strip of land that is the only land-based entry. Spain maintained the so-called 'garlic wall' for twelve years and despite the fact land entry to the Rock has long since been restored many of the workers here, formerly Spanish, are now Moroccan.

Britain in general and the Royal Navy in particular have made good use of Gib's strategic position, not only during the Napoleonic Wars but during both World Wars which followed. In World War II, the Rock was an invaluable base used in the support of innumerable Mediterranean convoys involved in the North African and Italian campaigns, and over the years it has earned for itself Britain's lasting gratitude. And the bond is two-ways: in a relatively recent referendum, the population voted overwhelmingly in favour of continued British involvement, external pressure notwithstanding.

With its modest dimensions, excellent road signs and English the common language, it is an ideal place for self-discovery. The fact that Marks & Spencer sits serenely in the high street alongside British Home Stores and Safeway does, I suppose, give one sense of security as well!

Apart from its well known strategic value, it is also well known for another element of its population – the Barbary Apes which live here in a carefully protected environment. Speaking of them, Churchill once said *"....as long as there are apes on the Rock, the British will be in Gibraltar"* and stories have it that once, when the ape population was in serious jeopardy, members of the British diplomatic community were despatched in haste to North Africa, there to capture sufficient animals to bolster the dwindling numbers, and the apes have thrived and been protected here ever since!

Your ship will berth at the Cruise Terminal which is pleasant and functional, if not beautiful. Inside, it is equipped with the facilities that you would expect – Post Office, souvenirs stalls, a newspaper stall (English newspapers almost current!) and an internet café.

The Terminal is a fifteen minute flat walk into town, but it does get rather hot, so please bear this in mind when making your decision about walking. Mini-buses run almost continuously from the terminal to Casemates Square, at the entrance to Main Street, and if you share with two or three others and fill the bus the fare works out at about a pound each.

Casemates Square is quite an attractive place, with pavement cafes, gift shops galore and a Tourist Information Centre immediately on your right hand as you enter the Square.

As we'll see a little later, Gibraltar is a shoppers paradise, and this might be a good place to pause and refresh yourselves before tackling the serious business of bargain hunting in the town proper! The principal artery is called Main Street, and this runs from Casemates Square to the Southport Gates. There is a Health Centre at the Casemates Square end of the Street, and the main Post Office is three blocks along on the right-hand-side. For much of its length it is pedestrianised (delivery vehicles excepted), but in the vicinity of the Cathedral traffic flows once more, so do tread wearily.

About half way along on the right you'll come across Old City Hall – slightly set back from the road, it has pavement cafes and flower seller stalls in front of it, and its quite a pleasant place to pause to watch the world go by. Opposite stands the Catholic Cathedral of St. Mary the Crowned, and then a little further, on the right, the Protestant Cathedral of the Holy Trinity.

Gibraltar's Government House is called the Convent, and is home to the Royal Gibraltar Regiment. It's located beyond Cathedral Square on the right hand side, with the Gun Room, flanked by two imposing brass cannons, on the opposite side of the road.

Nearby on the right you'll find King's Chapel which is deceptive, for it looks small and insignificant on the outside but is in fact quite large and imposing inside, so is worth a visit. Still walking southwards you'll pass through the Southport Gates where the South Bastion is on your right and Trafalgar cemetery on your left: here the gravestones stand in the serried ranks, mute testament to the many who fell at Trafalgar, that most bloody yet decisive of naval conflicts.

Cape Trafalgar, after which the battle is named, lies not far away and it was there, in October 1805, that Viscount Lord Nelson defeated Admiral Pierre Villeneuve, and died in the process. Nelson's body was brought here before being sent home, and today's visitor to the cemetery cannot help but be moved by the memory of this mighty conflict which did so much to thwart Napoleon's ambitions

A few hundred yards beyond the cemetery you'll find the lower cable car station and no visit to Gibraltar would be complete without a ride to the top but I'll talk about that in a few minutes. For the moment, let's stay in the heart of the town. Just off Main Street, in Bomb House Lane, you'll find the Gibraltar Museum which really is well worth a visit, for it provides a wealth of well presented information on this fascinating and truly historic place

Drop down to seaward off Main Street to Line Wall Road with its view across the harbour. In days of old this was a strategic spot, as the cannon that line the road testify. Heading northwards along Line Wall Road you'll reach the British War Memorial, with the back-end of City Hall next on the right standing behind some rather imposing gates. From here it is a hop, skip and a jump back to the bustling heart of Main Street.

Since we're still in the heart of the town a word about shopping: Gibraltar is a duty-free port and a paradise for the shopaholics amongst you – here you'll find treasures from many of the corners of the earth, and most things are competitively priced and of international quality. Cameras, cigarettes, alcohol are excellent buys as are lace, perfumes, watches and all sorts of other goodies. Shops are generally open between 9 am and 7.30 pm weekdays, and the local traders know full well when your ship is schedculed to be in town and will usually open up for you, even over week-ends – they never miss an opportunity!

I've already said that you'll find Marks & Spencer, large as life in the very centre, and British Homes Stores, Safeway and other household name stores are here as well.

By this time you might be feeling hot and thirsty – fear not. There are pubs galore in Main Street, and some of them look like your own local at home!

Currency is the Gibraltar Pound, par with Sterling, and there are any number of Banks and Bureaux de Change in Main Street.

That more or less exhausts the sights that are within easy walking distance, so lets consider some of the other things that you can do independently – by mini-bus, taxi, or by cable car.

Earlier I said that no visit to Gibraltar would be complete without a ride up to the top of the rock, and I've told you how to find the lower cable car station. The cable way runs more or less continuously throughout the day, but remember to check the timing of the last car up/down: it's an awful long walk! The views are spectacular – of the harbour, the town, the Spanish coast and across the straits to Ceuta, the Spanish enclave in Morocco.

At the upper station there is a restaurant and bar, near to the highest point of the rock which is called O'Hara's Battery. You can walk to it from the cable station, but do remember that the nature of Gibraltar's terrain means that parts of the pathways are steep and rocky, so if walking's your thing, wear sensible shoes.

This is the domain of the tail-less Barbary Macaques, those apes which are also found in Morocco and Algeria. About 160 of them live in Gibraltar and they are protected. In them you'll have a rare opportunity to see semi-wild primates at close quarters, but be warned: they can be quite cheeky, so keep your distance (and keep your valuables safe!).

At the beginning of this chapter I reminded you that Gibraltar is a small place, and by taxi you can see practically everything for yourselves: Europa Point, Nelson's Anchorage, the Alameda Botanical Gardens, the Moorish Castle, Parson's Lodge, the City-Under-Siege Exhibition and the Ibrahim-Al-Ibrahim Mosque.

If you want to swim you have the choice of three popular beaches – Eastern Beach, Catalan Bay and Sandy Bay, and the gourmets (and the hungry!) amongst you may want to try one of several good restaurants, ranging from Italian to Indian, Spanish and traditional British – even Fish & Chips!

But, to get the best out of your visit, do consider the tours that your ship is offering as they are designed to provide you with as wide a scope for sight-seeing as possible.

Undoubtedly there will be a 'Rock Tour; which will offer boundless photo opportunities. By mini-bus, this will probably involve minimal walking and will take you to St, Michael's Cave (where there are 75 steps to negotiate, nonetheless), then to the Ape's Den. This one may also include the Great Siege Tunnels, that marvellous feat of engineering which produced one of the best ever defensive systems ever created.

Catering for the fit and energetic, there may be a Cable Car and Walking Tour of the upper rock. In this case you'll ride the cableway to the top, possibly stopping off at the half-way point to enable you to get close up and personal with the apes in their den, then be guided along the several routes that trace the upper rock. Obviously, wear sensible shoes for this one. That journey back may be by mini-bus, which could take you for a whistle stop at the Moorish Castle where you'll seer the Tower of Homage, the most significant part of the castle still standing.

Another tour will take you out into the bay to see the dolphins, which live here in large numbers. You'll have the opportunity to capture these graceful, playful, creatures on film and this excursion is surely a must for those who want to commune with nature. Three species of dolphin are found here – the Common, the Striped and the Bottle-Nosed, and all of which breed in the sheltered bay that you'll be sailing across. If you're really lucky, you'll see the babies swimming along with the mothers.

Most of the tours that are offered here give you the choice of staying on in town at the end of the tour rather than going directly back to the ship, so if you want to indulge in some shopping after enjoying all the sights, then this is the option for you. Remember, though, if you leave the tour do ensure that you get back to the ship on time, because she won't wait for you!

Gibraltar is so much more than simply a shoppers' paradise: it has a wealth of history, spectacular scenery and (usually) wonderful weather.

You'll enjoy it!

AFTERWORD

You've left Gibraltar behind and have felt a pang of sadness as your ship turns her bows westward, outbound into the Atlantic once more.

Soon you'll have Cape St. Vincent, the southwestern-most point of mainland Europe on your starboard beam and you'll turn north, bound for the Bay and home. But, don't be sad – there is always the next cruise, and it'll only be a matter of months before those glossy brochures describing the delights of next year's itineraries hit your doormats, and the whole exciting business of choosing a cruise starts all over again.

In the meantime, there is time to enjoy a day or two at sea, chatting with new found friends and reliving your many experiences. Many lines take this opportunity to stage the Passenger Talent Show – and even if YOU are not so inclined, do go and watch your fellow passengers – I guarantee that you'll be amazed!

Then, on the last 'formal' night you'll probably experience the Baked Alaska Parade in the Restaurant, almost always followed by tearful renderings of 'Auld Lang Syne'.

All packed and with your suitcases left outside your cabin as you go to bed on the last night (don't forget to leave out the things you want to wear tomorrow!), you'll wake up in Dover, or Southampton, or wherever. Your cruise is over for now – but tomorrow is indeed another day.

The Mediterranean is, of course, a big place with dozens of ports and I'd have to write a very big book indeed if I set out to cover them all. The itinerary and the ports that I've described is representative of many a Mediterranean cruise, and I've really enjoyed talking you through it.

Thank you for joining me: in anticipation of next year and in the words of the late and much lamented Bob Haines, long-time Cruise Director of "Queen Elizabeth 2": 'Have a Nice Cruise!'

ACKNOWLEDGEMENTS

In the course of preparing the port presentations upon which these chapters are based, I have gleaned information from countless brochures, leaflets and guides: I am indebted to their authors and publishers, whoever they may be.

I have also consulted many other works, including:

"The Voyages of Columbus"	*Rex and Thea Rienits, Hamlyn*
"Discovering the New World"	*Theodore de Bry, London Editions*
"Journeys of the Great Explorers"	*Burton, Cavendish & Stonehouse AA Publishing*
"Life in the Age of Exploration"	*Reader's Digest*
"Columbus and the Age of Discovery"	*Zvi Dor-Ner, Harper Collins*
"The Triumph of the West"	*John Roberts, BBC Books*
"A World too Vast"	*A. McKee, Souvenir Press*
"The Life and Times of Columbus"	*Cesar Giardini, Hamlyn*
"Dubrovnik – a History"	*Robin Harris, Saqi*
"Florence"	*Edmund Swinglehurst, Coombe*
"Florence, Siena, Pisa and Lucca"	*Dana Facaros & Michael Pauls, Cadogan City Guides*
"Mediterranean Cruising"	*Insight Guides*
"Cruising around the Mediterranean"	*Thomas Cooke*
"Groc's Companion Guide to the Greek Islands"	*Geoffrey O'Connell*
"Lisbon – Mini Rough Guide"	*Matthew Hancock*
"Columbus – for Gold, God and Glory"	*Dyson, Hodder & Stoughton*
"In Search of Columbus"	*Hunter Davies, Sinclair-Stevenson*

I've benefited from many conversations and shared experiences with other 'Port Lecturers' and, finally, I've had the benefit of the extensive professional editorial experience of my son Mark, and from his valued colleague Susan Wright, herself a confirmed cruiser.

I am grateful to you all.

===============================